CASAS
TEST PREP
STUDENT
BOOK

FOR
MATH GOALS FORM
918 M LEVEL C/D

Preparing Adult Students for CASAS Math GOALS Tests
and for Workforce Entrance Math Exams

By Coaching for Better Learning, LLC

CASAS TEST PREP

STUDENT BOOK FOR MATH GOALS

FORM 918 M LEVEL C/D

Preparing Adult Students
for CASAS Math GOALS Tests
and for Workforce Entrance Math Exams

COACHING FOR BETTER LEARNING

TABLE OF CONTENT

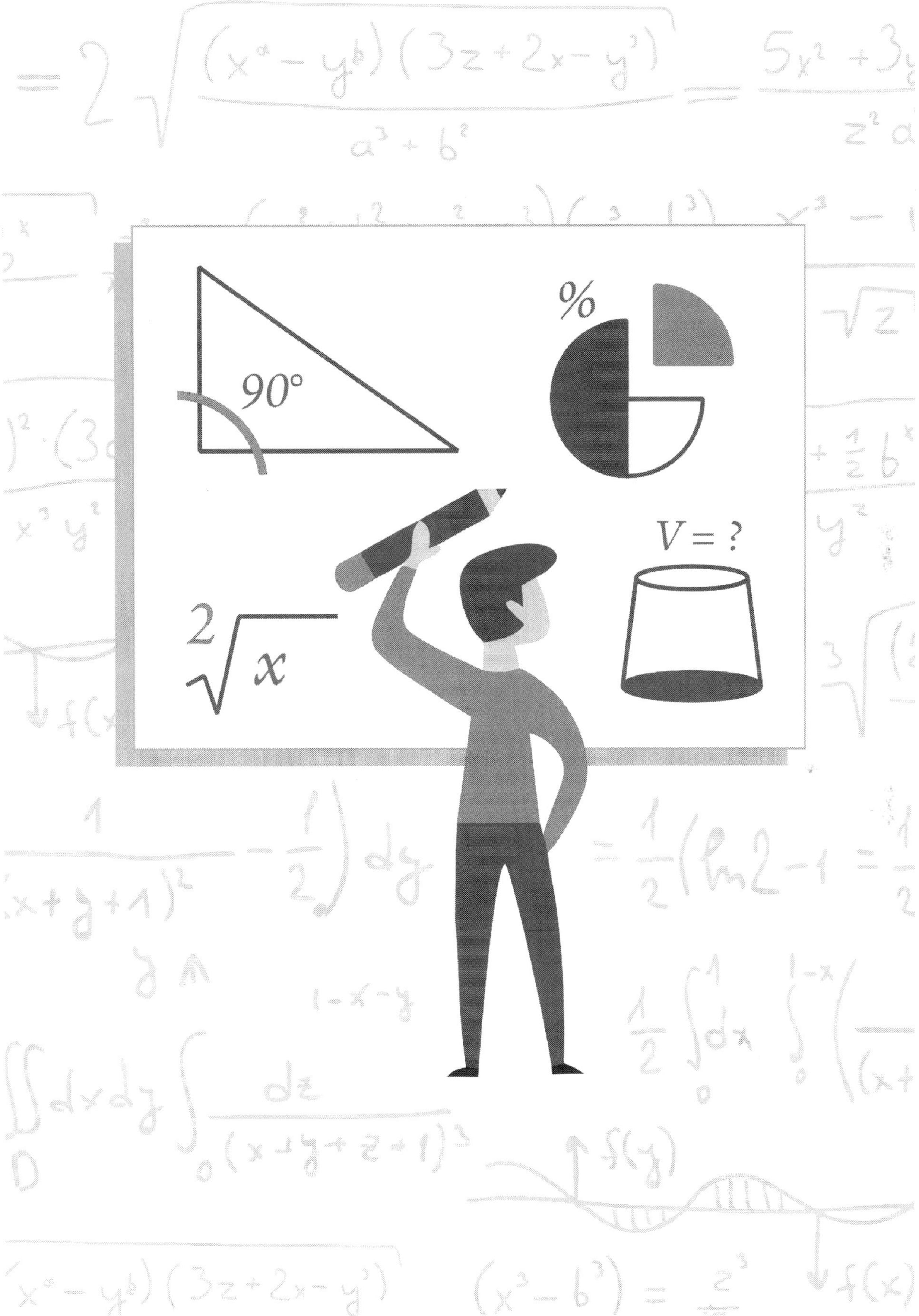
90°
%
V = ?

INTRODUCTION

This CASAS Test Prep student math textbook is designed to help teachers prepare adult students for the CASAS Math GOALS Test Form 918M Level C/D and for workforce and vocational training entrance math tests.

The content of this textbook is aligned with CASAS Competencies, with College and Career Readiness (CCR) and National Reporting System (NRS) standards and follows the CASAS GOALS Math Form 918M test blueprint.

In other words, this math textbook presents learning activities that help adult education programs, workforce programs, and their adult students to meet the Workforce Innovation and Opportunity Act (WIOA) math expectations.

This CASAS test prep textbook offers

- Seven (7) main chapters that cover NRS, CASAS and CCR standards and content such as

  1) **NUMBER AND OPERATIONS**

  2) **OPERATIONS AND ALGEBRAIC THINKING**

  3) **NUMBER AND OPERATIONS: FRACTIONS**

  4) **MEASUREMENT AND DATA**

  5) **GEOMETRY**

  6) **STATISTICS, DATA ANALYSIS, AND PROBABILITY**

  7) **PRACTICE TESTS AND ANSWER KEYS**

- Step-by-step instruction, plus practice exercises and answer keys

- Questions and tasks that encourage pair work, group work, and classroom discussion on math ideas and concepts

- Real-world word problems and key concepts

- Two (2) practice tests that mimic the CASAS Math GOALS Form 918 M test format and rigor, plus answer keys

Specifically, this textbook allows math teachers to provide learners with the space and time to experiment with math concepts and ideas and to get deeper into their learning process. For example, the tasks presented in this book aim to

- Make learners think more deeply about math structure and concepts and therefore improve their mathematical thinking skills
- Provide learners with hands-on tasks relevant to their situation
- Help learners connect their math learning with the real world
- Create opportunities for learners to read about, write about, and discuss math ideas and concepts
- Invite learners to reflect on their learning

Therefore, we encourage math teachers and students NOT to use this textbook as a collection of worksheets. Rather, for effective use of this resource, we highly recommend that learners have a safe classroom environment where they can collaborate with their classmates.

The use will be more productive if students are in a learner-centered classroom where they can learn to appreciate the beauty of math, experiment with math ideas, make mistakes and take risks, discuss their work and methods, and articulate their understanding of math ideas and concepts without the fear of being judged.

In a nutshell, this CASAS Test prep math textbook covers more than the basic content that learners need to master so they can perform very well on the CASAS Math GOALS Form 918 M test.

Now that you know what's in the textbook, let's get to work. Enjoy the journey!

CHAPTER 1: NUMBER AND OPERATIONS

KEY VOCABULARY

multi-digit integers, multiplication, division, percent, fraction, decimal, rational number, ratio

Multiply and Divide Multi-digit Integers and Decimal Numbers

We can solve problem situations that require multiplying and dividing with multi-digit positive integers and decimal numbers, carry out the computation accurately, and interpret the answer in context.

Example. A company took 148 employees to a management conference across the country. Each round-trip plane ticket cost $632.35. What was the total amount spent to take the employees to the conference?

Step 1. Notice that this is a multiplication problem. Multiply 632.35 x 148

Step 2. Ignore the decimal points and multiply the numbers as whole numbers:

$$
\begin{array}{r}
63235 \times \\
148 \\
\hline
505880 + \\
252940 \\
63235 \\
\hline
9358780
\end{array}
$$

Step 3. Place the decimal point. Notice that 632.35 has **two** decimal digits. Thus, the product will have **two** decimal digits:

93,587.<u>80</u>

Step 4. So, the total amount needed to take the employees to the conference is **$93,587.80**

Example. How many hours are there in 2,040 minutes?

Step 1. We know that there are 60 minutes in 1 hour. Divide $2,040 \div 60$:

$$
\begin{array}{r}
34 \\
60\overline{)2040} \\
\underline{180} \\
240 \\
\underline{240} \\
0
\end{array}
$$

Step 2. Thus, there are **34 hours** in 2,040 minutes.

Percent

Percent means "**out of 100**." We can use the percent symbol (%) as a way to write a fraction with a common denominator of 100. For example, instead of saying "19 out of 100animals are cats," we can say "19% of animals are cats."

In other words:

$$\textbf{19\% means } \frac{19}{100}$$

A percent can also be expressed as a **fraction or decimal.** To convert a fraction to a percent, divide the top number (numerator) by the bottom number (denominator), then multiply the result by 100, and add the "%" sign.

Example. Convert $\frac{1}{5}$ to a percent.

Step 1. Divide 1 by 5:

$$1 \div 5 = 0.2$$

Step 2. Multiply the result by 100:

$$0.2 \times 100 = 20$$

Step 3. Add the "%" sign: 20%:

Step 4. Thus, we have:

$$\frac{1}{5} = \mathbf{20\%}$$

Example. Convert 80% to a fraction.

Step 1. We know that:

$$80\% = \frac{80}{100}$$

Step 2. Simplify the fraction:

$$\frac{80}{100} = \frac{8}{10} = \frac{4}{5}$$

To convert from decimal to percent, we multiply by 100, and add the % sign.

Example. Convert 0.43 to a percent.

Step 1. Multiply 0.43 x 100:

$$0.43 \times 100 = 43$$

(Recall: To multiply by 100 means to **move the decimal point 2 places to the right**.)

Step 2. Add the % sign:

$$0.43 = \mathbf{43\%}$$

Example. Convert 9% to a decimal.

Step 1. We know that:

$$9\% = \frac{9}{100}$$

Step 2. Divide 9 by 100:

$$\frac{9}{100} = 0.09$$

(Recall: To divide by 100 is to **move the decimal point 2 places to the left**.)

Step 3. So, 9% = **0.09**

We can solve problems using percent or calculate a missing value from a percent relationship.

Example. John scored 36 out of 60 in a math test. What percent was that?

Step 1. We can write John's score as a fraction:

$$36 \text{ out of } 60 = \frac{36}{60}$$

Step 2. Divide 36 by 60:

$$\frac{36}{60} = 0.6$$

Step 3. Multiply the result by 100:

$$0.6 \times 100 = 60$$

Step 4. Add the % sign.

Step 5. So, John's score was **60%**.

Ratios

We use ratios to make comparisons between two quantities. Look at the following figures:

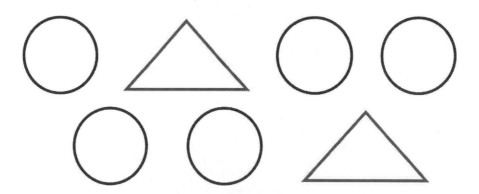

We can write the ratio of triangles to circles in different ways:

Use the **(:)** to separate the numbers: **2:5**

Use the word "to": **2 to 5**

> Write it like a fraction: $\dfrac{2}{5}$

When two ratios are equal, we have a **proportion**:

$$\frac{2}{5} = \frac{8}{20}$$

$$\frac{10}{60} = \frac{1}{6}$$

Notice that these two fractions are **equivalent**.

Example. Jack bought 72apples for $27. How many apples can Jack buy if he has $3?

Step 1. Let x be the number of apples.

Step 2. Write the proportion that represents the problem:

$$\frac{72}{27} = \frac{x}{3}$$

Step 3. Apply the cross product:

$$\frac{72}{27} = \frac{x}{3}$$

$$27x = 72 \cdot 3$$

Step 4. Solve the equation:

$$27x = 216$$

$$27x = 216 \implies x = \frac{216}{27} = 8$$

Step 5. So, Jack can buy **8 apples**.

Rational Numbers

A rational number is a number that can be written as a **ratio**. In other words, a rational number can be written as a **fraction** in which both the numerator and the denominator are whole numbers. Positive and negative numbers, fractions, and decimals are all rational numbers.

Rational Numbers

$$8.376 \qquad -56 \qquad \frac{8}{13} \qquad 2{,}097$$

Addition and subtraction of rational numbers

Addition and subtraction of rational numbers is done in the same way as that of the addition and subtraction of **fractions**. When adding and subtracting fractions, consider two cases: when the denominator is the same and when the denominator is different.

Example. Add $\dfrac{5}{6} + \dfrac{3}{4}$

Step 1. Note that we have different denominators. To add them, we must express both fractions as the sum of equivalent fractions with the same denominator.

Step 2. Multiply the numerator and denominator of the first fraction by 2 and multiply the numerator and denominator of the second fraction by 3:

$$\frac{5 \times 2}{6 \times 2} = \frac{10}{12}$$

$$\frac{3 \times 3}{4 \times 3} = \frac{9}{12}$$

Step 3. Now we have fractions with the same denominator. To add fractions with the same denominator, keep the same denominator and add the numerators:

$$\frac{10}{12} + \frac{9}{12} = \frac{19}{12}$$

Step 4. Thus, we have:

$$\frac{5}{6} + \frac{3}{4} = \frac{19}{12}$$

We can also add a decimal or subtract a decimal from a fraction. We can do this in two ways: convert the decimal to a fraction or convert the fraction to a decimal. Then we add fractions to fractions or decimals to decimals.

Example. Subtract $1.25 - \frac{3}{4}$

Step 1. Convert 1.25 to a fraction. Rewrite the decimal divided by 1:

$$\frac{1.25}{1}$$

Step 2. Multiply both the numerator and denominator by **100** because there are 2 digits after the decimal point:

$$\frac{1.25 \times 100}{1 \times 100} = \frac{125}{100}$$

Step 3. Simplify the fraction:

$$\frac{125}{100} = \frac{25}{20} = \frac{5}{4}$$

(Divide the numerator and denominator by 5 twice.)

Step 4. Subtract both fractions. Notice that we have the same denominator:

$$\frac{5}{4} - \frac{3}{4} = \frac{2}{4}$$

Step 5. Simplify the fraction:

$$\frac{2}{4} = \frac{1}{2}$$

Step 6. So, the result is:

$$1.25 - \frac{3}{4} = \frac{1}{2}$$

Multiplication and division of rational numbers

We multiply and divide rational numbers the same way we multiply and divide **fractions**.

Example. Multiply $\frac{7}{10} \; x \; \frac{5}{2}$

Step 1. Multiply the numerators and the denominators:

$$\frac{7}{10} \; x \; \frac{5}{2} = \frac{35}{20}$$

Step 2. Simplify the fraction:

$$\frac{35}{20} = \frac{7}{4}$$

Step 3. So, the result is:

$$\frac{7}{10} \; x \; \frac{5}{2} = \frac{7}{4}$$

We can also multiply and divide a fraction to a decimal. We can do this in two ways: convert the decimal to a fraction or convert the fraction to a decimal.

Example. Divide $\frac{2}{5} \div 2.4$

Step 1. Convert 2.4 to a fraction. Rewrite the decimal divided by 1:

$$\frac{2.4}{1}$$

Step 2. Multiply both the numerator and denominator by **10** because there is 1 digit after the decimal point:

$$\frac{2.4 \; x \; 10}{1 \; x \; 10} = \frac{24}{10}$$

Step 3. Simplify the fraction:

$$\frac{24}{10} = \frac{12}{5}$$

Step 4. Divide the fractions. To divide fractions, take **the reciprocal** (invert the fraction) of the divisor and multiply the dividend:

$$\frac{2}{5} \div \frac{12}{5}$$

Step 5. Multiply the first fraction by **the reciprocal** of the second fraction:

$$\frac{2}{5} \; x \; \frac{5}{12} = \frac{10}{60}$$

Step 6. Simplify the fraction:

$$\frac{10}{60} = \frac{1}{6}$$

Step 7. Thus, the result is:

$$\frac{2}{5} \div 2.4 = \frac{1}{6}$$

Practice Exercises

1) There are 3,595 pieces in a jigsaw puzzle. How many pieces are there in 18 puzzles?

   A. 63,720
   B. 65,090
   C. 64,990
   D. 64,710

2) How many gallons are there in 4,664 pints?   Hint: 1 gallon = 8 pints

   A. 583 gallons
   B. 684 gallons
   C. 593 gallons
   D. 995 gallons

3) If Paul runs 1.76 miles every day, how many miles can he run in three weeks?

   A. 5.28 miles
   B. 36.96 miles
   C. 24.78 miles
   D. 6.38 miles

4) Which of the following is equivalent to 45%?

   A. 1/5
   B. 9/20
   C. 3/5
   D. 3/20

5) Which of the following is equivalent to 0.11?

   A. 11/10
   B. 11%
   C. 10/11
   D. 1.1%

6) A car can travel 380 miles on a full tank of gas. A more efficient car can travel 25% further. How many miles *further* can the efficient car travel on a tank?

   A. 95 miles
   B. 76 miles
   C. 82 miles
   D. 90 miles

7) Exactly 8% of the cost of a smartphone was tax. If the tax was $34, what was the cost of the smartphone?

   A. $391
   B. $415
   C. $520
   D. $425

8) In a bag of blue and white cards, the ratio of blue cards to white cards is 5:8. If the bag contains 65blue cards, how many white cards are there?

   A. 80
   B. 96
   C. 104
   D. 122

9) Jane fills her gas tank with 8 gallons of gas for a cost of $14.5. How much would it costs to fill a 12-gallon tank?

   A. $21.75
   B. $29.00
   C. $30.50
   D. $19.85

10) Kelly can make 9 pairs of earrings in one week. Assuming she works at this constant rate, how many complete pairs of earrings can she make in 12 days?

   A. 18 pairs
   B. 15 pairs
   C. 16 pairs
   D. 20 pairs

11) What is the result of $4.2 + \frac{1}{8}$?

   A. 5.594
   B. 5.165
   C. 4.825
   D. 4.325

12) What is the result of $\frac{3}{10} + \frac{2}{5}$?

   A. 7/5
   B. 7/10
   C. 1/10
   D. 3/5

13) Divide $60 \div \frac{3}{4}$.

    A. 80
    B. 15
    C. 45
    D. 65

14) Multiply$3.6 \times \frac{10}{3}$.

    A. 8.6
    B. 19/3
    C. 12
    D. 13/2

15) Which of the following is true?

    A. 50% = 50/10
    B. 0.9 = 9%
    C. 1/5 = 20%
    D. 10% = 1/100

ANSWER KEYS

1) D	6) A	11) D
2) A	7) D	12) B
3) B	8) C	13) A
4) B	9) A	14) C
5) B	10) B	15) C

REFLECTION ON LEARNING

Answer the following reflection questions and feel free to discuss your responses with a classmate.

- What math idea, principle, or structure did you learn from this section?

_____

_____

_____

_____

- What math concepts did you learn?

_____

_____

_____

- What procedures or method did you work on in this section?

_____

_____

_____

- What aspect of this section is still not 100% clear for you?

_____

_____

_____

- What else do you want your teacher to know?

_____

_____

_____

$$\sqrt[x]{2x} = ?$$

$$(x + 3) + x$$

$$\sqrt[2]{x}$$

CHAPTER 2: OPERATIONS AND ALGEBRAIC THINKING

KEY VOCABULARY

variable, algebraic expression, equation, formula, dependent and independent variable, graph, sequence

Variables and Algebraic Expressions

A **variable** is a symbol for a number we don't know yet. It is usually a letter like **x** or **y**, but we can use any letter.

An **algebraic expression** is an expression involving numbers, fractions, parentheses, operation signs and letters that becomes a number when numbers are substituted for the letters.

Examples of Algebraic Expressions

$$2x - 6y \qquad 5a^2 - 6b + 9 \qquad \frac{x}{6} + 5z$$

Algebraic expressions are useful because they represent the value of an expression for all the values a variable can take on. When we describe an expression in words that includes a variable, we are describing an algebraic expression: an expression with a variable.

Example. Write an expression for "50% of a number."

Step 1. Let x be the number. We know that 50% is equivalent to ½.

Step 2. Find the 50% of x:

$$50\% \; of \; x = \frac{1}{2}x$$

Example. Write an expression for "The product of a number and the same number less 8."

   Step 1. Let n be the number. The number less 8 is:

$$x - 8$$

   Step 2. So, the product of the number and the same number less 8 is:

$$x \cdot (x - 8)$$

Equations

An equation is a mathematical statement that two things are equal. In an equation, the left side is always equal to the right side. The most common equations contain one or more **variables**.

$$3x + 17 = 51$$

To solve an equation, follow these steps:

   Step 1. Figure out what to remove to get the value of the variable.
   Step 2. To remove a number, add its opposite to both sides.
   We can solve word problems using equations with a letter for the **unknown number** to represent the problem, simple contextual math situations, or real-life and mathematical problems.

Example. Last summer, Jen charges people $7.5 per hour for babysitting and $9 for going to their house. If she makes $39 one day, how many hours did Jen spend babysitting?

   Step 1. Let x be the number of hours.

   Step 2. If Jen works x hours, then she charges 7.5x dollars.

   Step 3. Write the equation that represents the problem:

$$7.5x + 9 = 39$$

   Step 4. Solve the equation:

$$7.5x + 9 = 39$$

$$7.5x = 39 - 9$$

$$7.5x = 30 \implies x = \frac{30}{7.5} = 4$$

   Step 5. So, the number of hours Jen spent babysitting was **4 hours**.

Using algebraic concepts and terminology, we can solve computationally and conceptually challenging multistep problems.

Example. The sum of three consecutive numbers is 108. What is the smallest of the three numbers?

Step 1. Let x be the smallest number.

Step 2. The three consecutive numbers can be represented by x, $x + 1$, $x + 2$. So, we can set up the equation that describes the problem:

$$x + x + 1 + x + 2 = 108$$

Step 3. Solve the equation:

$$x + x + 1 + x + 2 = 108$$

$$3x + 3 = 108$$

$$3x = 108 - 3$$

$$3x = 105 \implies x = \frac{105}{3} = 35$$

Step 4. So, the smallest number is **35**

Step 5. Check the result. The three consecutive numbers are 35, 36, and 37.

The sum of 35 + 36 + 37 = **108**

Formulas

A formula is a relationship expressed using numbers and mathematical symbols. A formula usually has an equal sign (=) and two or more **variables**. A formula shows us how variables are related to each other. For example, the formula of the acceleration of an object is given by:

$$a = \frac{\Delta v}{t}$$

Where a represents acceleration, Δv represents change in the velocity and has units of meters per second (m/s), and t represents the time in which the change occurs and has units of seconds(s). Notice that there are three variables (a, Δv, t) in the previous formula.

We can rearrange formulas to isolate specific variables to solve problems involving life-skill-related and technical formulas.

Example. The formula for converting a measurement in Fahrenheit to Kelvin is

$$F = 1.8K - 459.67$$

Where F is the temperature in degrees Fahrenheit and K is the temperature in degrees Kelvin. If the temperature is 59 degrees Fahrenheit, what is it in Kelvin?

Step 1. We know that F = 59. Put this value in the formula:

$$59 = 1.8K - 459.67$$

Step 2. We have an equation. Solve the equation for K:

$$59 = 1.8K - 459.67$$

$$1.8K = 59 + 459.67$$

$$1.8K = 518.67 \implies k = \frac{518.67}{1.8} = 288.15$$

Step 3. Thus, 59 degrees Fahrenheit = **288.15 degrees Kelvin**.

Dependent and Independent Variables

An **independent variable** is a variable that represents a quantity that is being manipulated in a situation. The letter x is often the variable used to represent the dependent variable in an equation.

A **dependent variable** represents a quantity whose value depends on how the independent variable is manipulated. The letter y is often the variable used to represent the dependent variable in an equation:

Dependent variable

$$y = 3x - 8$$

Independent variable

Typically, when we graph an equation, we put the independent variable on the **x-axis** and the dependent variable on the **y-axis**. We can use a graph to answer questions about functional relationships between independent and dependent variables.

Example. The graph below shows how the amount of time a receptionist spends on the phone is related to the number of phone calls she routes to employees. If the receptionist routes 40 phone calls, how much time will she have spent on the phone in total?

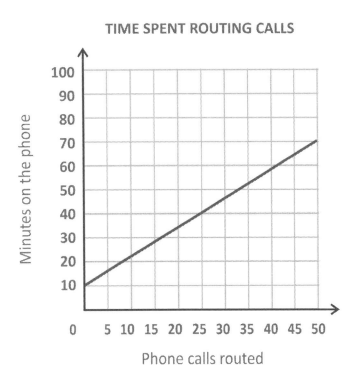

Step 1. Find 40 phone calls on the *x*-axis. Move up the line until you intersect the graph. (Notice that phone calls are the independent variable.)

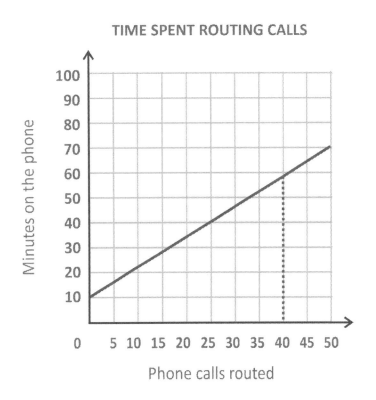

Step 2. Now move left until you intersect the *y*-axis:

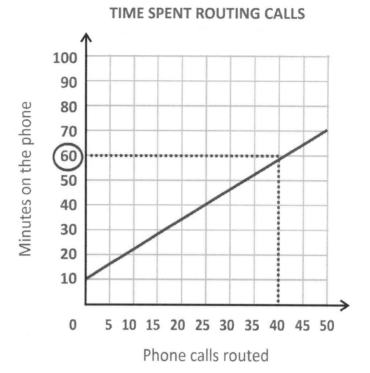

TIME SPENT ROUTING CALLS

Step 3. Note that the y-intercept is at 60 minutes.

Step 4. So, the receptionist will have spent a total of **60 minutes** on the phone.

Numbers Sequence

A sequence is a set of numbers (or other objects) that usually follow a **pattern**. The individual elements in a sequence are called **terms**. For example, notice the patterns:

NUMBER SEQUENCE	PATTERN
40, 80, 120, 160,...	Add 40
5,000, 500, 50, 5,...	Subtract 10
1.5, 7.5, 37.5, 187.5,...	Multiply 5
4, 2, 1, 0.5,...	Divide by 2

Example. Find the missing term in the following sequence:

16, 4, 1, _____ , 0.0625, ...

Step 1. To find the missing term in a number sequence, first find the pattern of the number sequence. Note that each term in the number sequence is formed by divide the preceding number by 4

Step 2. So, the missing term is $1 \div 4 = $ **0.25**

PRACTICE EXERCISES

1)   Which algebraic expression represents the phrase, "The sum of two consecutive even numbers"?

    A. $x + (x + 2)$
    B. $x + 2x$
    C. $2x + (2x + 2)$
    D. $(x + 1) + (x + 2)$

2)   Which algebraic expression represents the phrase, "A number increased by 45%"?

    A.   0.45x
    B.   45x
    C.   4.5x
    D.   1.45x

3)   At a car rental agency, renting a car costs a one-time fee of $28.50 plus $0.85 for every mile it is driven. Which of the following equations would be correct if it costs Frank $120 to rent a car?

    A. $0.85x + 28.5 = 120$
    B. $28.5x + 0.85 = 120$
    C. $0.85 + 20.5 = 120x$
    D. $0.85x - 28.5 = 120$

4)   Earl received a paycheck of $531. This amount reflects his weekly earnings less 10% of his earnings for deductions. How much was Earl paid before deductions were taken out?

    A. $584.1
    B. $590
    C. $541
    D. $595.5

5)   The length of a rectangular door is 72 inches, and the perimeter is 200 inches. What is the width of the door?

    A.   28 inches
    B.   32 inches
    C.   25 inches
    D.   36 inches

6) A group of 328 people consists of men, women, and children. There are five times as many men as children and twice as many women as children. How many women are there?

   A. 41
   B. 93
   C. 82
   D. 85

7) The formula of the acceleration of an object is given by $a = \frac{\Delta v}{t}$, where a represents acceleration, Δv represents change in the velocity and has units of meters per second (m/s), and t represents the time in which the change occurs and has units of seconds (s). Which is an appropriate measurement unit for acceleration?

   A. m^2/s
   B. m/s^2
   C. s/m
   D. s/m^2

8) Ohm's Lawis used to calculate the relationship between voltage, current, and resistance in an electrical circuit. Ohm's Law is given by $V = I \times R$, where V is the voltage and has units of Volt (V), I is the current and has units of Ampere (A), and R is the resistance and has units of Ohm (Ω). If the current of an electrical circuit is 7.5 A and the voltage is 12 V, what is the resistance of the circuit?

   A.   0.625 Ω
   B.   90 Ω
   C.   16 Ω
   D.   1.6 Ω

9) The formula for converting a measurement in Celsius to Kelvin is: F = 1.8K − 459.67, where F is the temperature in degrees Fahrenheit and K is the temperature in degrees Kelvin. If the temperature is 300 degrees Kelvin, what is it in Fahrenheit?

   A.   98.56°F
   B.   494.30°F
   C.   80.33°F
   D.   101.10°F

The graph below shows how the amount of turkey George has left is related to the number of sandwiches he makes:

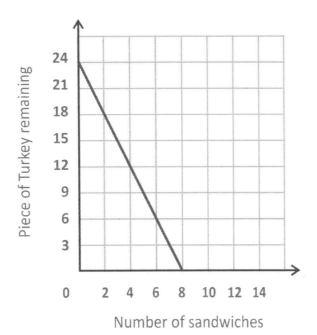

(Questions 10 to 12)

10) If George makes 4 sandwiches, how many pieces of turkey remain?

    A.   12
    B.   15
    C.   9
    D.   10

11) If George makes 8 sandwiches, how many pieces of turkey remain?

    A.   24
    B.   12
    C.   3
    D.   None

12) What is the independent variable?

    A.   Pieces of turkey remaining
    B.   Number of sandwiches
    C.   Number of sandwiches remaining
    D.   None of the above

13) The area of a trapezoid is given by $A = \frac{1}{2}(a + b)h$, where A is the area of the trapezoid, a and b are the lengths of each base, and h is the height. If the dimensions of a trapezoid are $a = 8$, $b = 9$, and $h = 18$, what is the area of the trapezoid?

A. 306
B. 153
C. 147
D. 85

14) What is the missing term in the following sequence?

1.2, 6, 30, ____ , 750, ...

A. 90.2
B. 120
C. 150
D. 550

15) What is the missing term in the following sequence?

6, 12, 48, 288, ____ , ...

A. 1,152
B. 2,304
C. 878
D. 1,896

ANSWER KEYS

1) C	6) C	11) D
2) D	7) B	12) B
3) A	8) D	13) D
4) B	9) C	14) C
5) A	10) A	15) B

REFLECTION ON LEARNING

Answer the following reflection questions and feel free to discuss your responses with a classmate.

- What math idea, principle, or structure did you learn from this section?

- What math concepts did you learn?

- What procedures or method did you work on in this section?

- What aspect of this section is still not 100% clear for you?

- What else do you want your teacher to know?

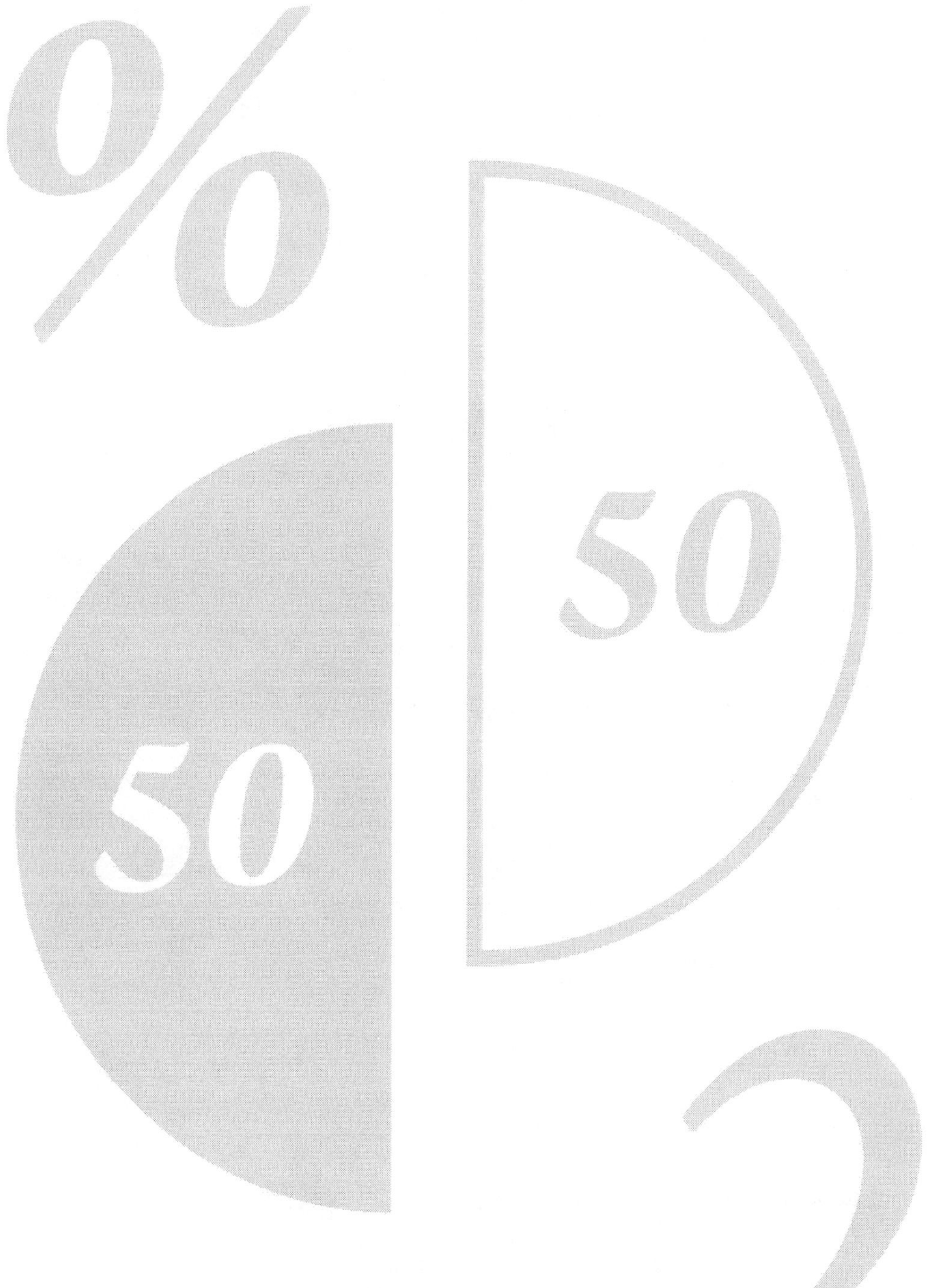
%
50
50
2

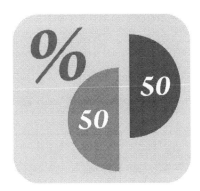

CHAPTER 3: NUMBER AND OPERATIONS: FRACTIONS

KEY VOCABULARY

ratio, proportion, proportional relationship

Ratios

A ratio is a statement of how two numbers or quantities compare. It is a comparison of the size of one number to the size of another number. Look at the following figures:

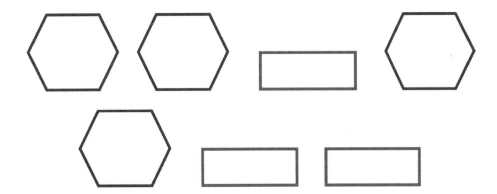

We can write the ratio of rectangles to hexagons in different ways:

Use the **(:)** to separate the numbers: **3 : 4**

Use the word "to": **3 to 4**

Write it like a fraction: $\frac{3}{4}$

When two ratios are equal, we have a **proportion**:

$$\frac{3}{4} = \frac{9}{12}$$

Notice that the previous fractions are equivalent.

Example. A bag contains 135 marbles, some red and some white. The ratio of red marbles to white ones is 2:7. How many red marbles are there?

Step 1. Let 2x and 7x be the numbers of red marbles and white marbles, respectively. Since the bag contains 135 marbles, we can set up the equation that represents the problem:

$$2x + 7x = 135$$

Step 2. Solve the equation:

$$2x + 7x = 135$$

$$9x = 135 \implies x = \frac{135}{9} = 15$$

Step 3. So, the number of red marbles is 2x = 2(15) = **30 marbles**.

Step 4. Check the result:

The number of white marbles is 7x = 7(15) = 105

Total number of marbles in the bag = 30 + 105 = **135**

Example. A certain dessert recipe calls for 3 pounds of sugar for every 12 pounds of flour. If 50 pounds of the dessert must be prepared, how much sugar is needed?

Step 1. Let x be the quantity of sugar required.

Step 2. Adding 3 pounds of sugar to 12 pounds of flour makes a total of 15 pounds of the dessert. So, the ratio of pounds of sugar to pounds of dessert is **3:15**

Step 3. Set up the proportion that represents the problem:

$$\frac{3}{15} = \frac{x}{50}$$

Step 4. Solve the equation:

$$\frac{3}{15} = \frac{x}{50}$$

$$15x = 150 \implies x = \frac{150}{15} = 10$$

Step 5. So, the quantity the sugar required is **10 pounds**.

Proportional Relationships

When two values always maintain **the same ratio**, forming the same fraction when we divide them, they have a **proportional relationship.**

Example. The following table shows the time it takes to ride the elevator to three different floors of a building:

Floor number	2	4	6
Time needed (in seconds)	5	10	15

Based on this table, is the floor number proportional to the time it takes to get there?

Step 1. Find the ratio to get to each floor.

Step 2. Write the ratio of floor 2 as a fraction:

$$\frac{2}{5}$$

Step 3. Write the ratio of floor 4 as a fraction:

$$\frac{4}{10} = \frac{2}{5} \ (simplest\ form)$$

Step 4. Write the ratio of floor 6 as a fraction:

$$\frac{6}{15} = \frac{2}{5} \ (simplest\ form)$$

Step 5. Notice that we get **the same ratio** (equivalent fractions). Thus, **the floor number is proportional to the time.**

PRACTICE EXERCISES

1) In a certain room, there are 36 women and 24 men. What is the ratio of women to the total number of people?

   A. 3/2
   B. 2/3
   C. 3/5
   D. 3/4

2) On a certain map, 1 inch = 15 miles in actual distance. If two places are 240 miles apart, what is their distance on the map?

   A. 16 inches
   B. 12 inches
   C. 15 inches
   D. 24 inches

3) If the ratio of chocolates to ice cream cones in a box is 5:7, and the number of chocolates is 40, how many ice cream cones are in the box?

   A. 70
   B. 50
   C. 64
   D. 56

4) A person types 180 words in 2 minutes. How much time does he take to type 900 words?

   A. 20 minutes
   B. 10 minutes
   C. 15 minutes
   D. 12 minutes

5) At Riverside School, there are 150 girls and 180 boys. The numbers of girls and boys at Richmond School are proportional to the numbers at Riverside School. Which of the following could be the numbers of girls and boys at Richmond School?

   A. Girls: 120, boys: 240
   B. Girls: 100, boys: 130
   C. Girls: 90, boys: 108
   D. Girls: 60, boys: 90

6) The table shows a proportional relationship between the ounces (oz.) of blue paint and ounces of yellow paint needed to make a certain shade of green. A row of values is missing in the table:

Blue (oz.)	Yellow (oz.)
6	13.8
10	23
8	18.4
?	?

Which of the following mixtures of paint could be used as the missing values in the table?

A. 17 oz. blue and 39.1 oz. yellow
B. 20 oz. blue and 44 oz. yellow
C. 5 oz. blue and 6.5 oz. yellow
D. 28 oz. blue and 67.2 oz. yellow

7) Christine drew a scale drawing of a house. A room in the house that is 15 feet wide in real life is 2.5 inches wide in the drawing. What is the scale of the drawing?

A. 1 inch = 5 feet
B. 2 feet = 80 inches
C. 1 inch = 6 feet
D. 3 inch = 30 feet

8) What is the missing value in the following table of equivalent ratios?

4.6	46
6	60
?	110

A. 10
B. 11
C. 9
D. 13

9) The following table shows Gary's earnings based on the number of hours he works:

Number of hours	3	4	6
Gary's earnings	$37.5	$50	$75

Are Gary's earnings proportional to the number of hours he works?

A. No
B. Yes
C. There is not enough information given.

10) The following table shows Emily's weight at different ages:

Age (in years)	4	10	15
Weight (kg)	20	50	60

Is Emily's weight proportional to her age?

A. Yes
B. No
C. There is not enough information given.

11) At the zoo, the ratio of monkeys to turtles is 6: b. There are48monkeys and 104 turtles at the zoo. What is the value of b?

A. 8
B. 14
C. 3
D. 13

12) 225 students want ice cream and 600 students want pizza. What is the ratio of the number of students who want ice cream to the number of students who want pizza?

A. 3:8
B. 4:5
C. 5:12
D. 2:3

13) Daisy took a total of 18 quizzes over the course of 6 weeks. After attending 14 weeks of school this quarter, how many quizzes will daisy have taken in total? Assume the relationship is directly proportional.

A. 36
B. 50
C. 42
D. 28

14) Jack bought nine watermelons for $27. How many watermelons can Jack buy if he has $96?

    A. 29
    B. 40
    C. 32
    D. 30

15) The currency in Japan is the yen. The exchange rate is approximately $1 = 110.4yen. At this rate, how many yen would we get if we exchanged $1,711.2?

    A. 15.5 yen
    B. 26.5 yen
    C. 18.3 yen
    D. 16.2 yen

Answer Keys

1) C	6) A	11) D
2) A	7) C	12) A
3) D	8) B	13) C
4) B	9) B	14) C
5) C	10) B	15) A

REFLECTION ON LEARNING

Answer the following reflection questions and feel free to discuss your responses with a classmate.

- What math idea, principle, or structure did you learn from this section?

_____

_____

_____

- What math concepts did you learn?

_____

_____

_____

- What procedures or method did you work on in this section?

_____

_____

_____

- What aspect of this section is still not 100% clear for you?

_____

_____

_____

- What else do you want your teacher to know?

_____

_____

_____

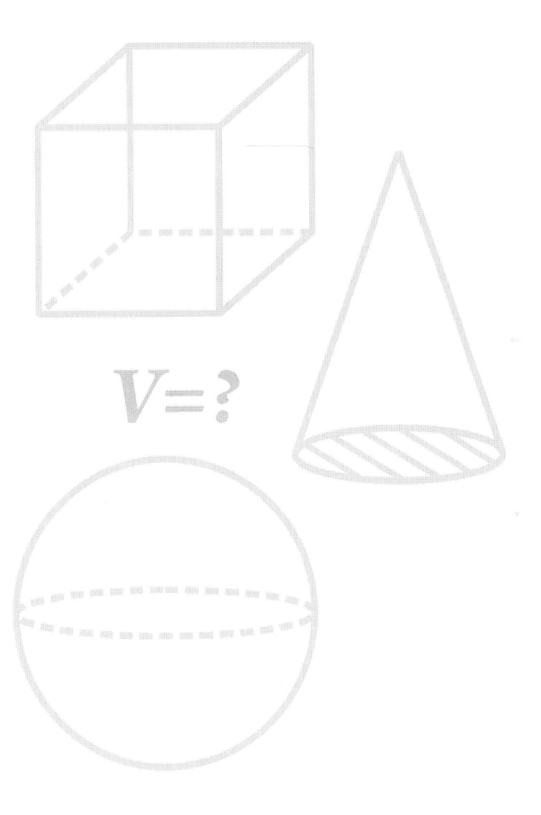

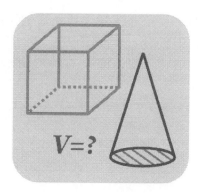

CHAPTER 4: MEASUREMENT AND DATA

KEY VOCABULARY

units of time, circumference, circle, area, volume, proportion, scale

Units of time

The basic units of time we are familiar with from the smallest unit to the greatest unit are **second, minute, hour, day, week, month,** and **year**. A second is the smallest unit of time. These units have the following relationships:

1 MINUTE = 60 SECONDS
1 HOUR = 60 MINUTES
1 DAY = 24 HOURS
1 WEEK = 7 DAYS
1 YEAR = 12 MONTHS
1 YEAR = 365 DAYS

We can calculate with and convert between units of time.

Example. How many hours are there in 1 year?

   Step 1. We know 1 year = 365 days, so we convert 365 days to hours.

Step 2. To convert larger units (days) to smaller units (hours), **multiply** the number of larger units by **24.** (Recall: 1 day = 24 hours)

> 365 days = 365 x 24hours = 8,760 hours

Step 3. So, there are**8, 760 hours** in a year.

Example. Convert 4,320 minutes to days.

Step 1. To convert smaller units (minutes) to larger units (days), **divide** the number of smaller units by **1,440. (**Recall: 1 day = 24 hours = 24 x 60 minutes = 1,440 minutes)

> $$4,320 \text{minutes} = \frac{4,320}{1,440} \text{days} = 3 \text{ days}$$

Step 2. So, 4,320 minutes = **3 days**.

Circumference and Circle

In a circle, all points are the same distance from the center. The distance between the center and the circle border is called **the radius**.

The line segment that has its endpoints on the circle and passes through the center is called **the diameter.** The distance around the circle is called **the circumference**.

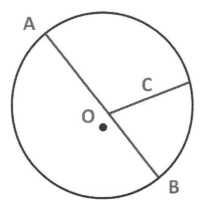

O = Center   OC = Radius   AB = Diameter

The circumference of a circle is found using the following formula:

> $$C = 2\pi \cdot r$$

Where C is the circumference of the circle, r is the radius of the circle, and $\pi \approx 3.14$

If we know the diameter of a circle, the circumference can be found using this formula:

$$C = \pi \cdot d$$

Where d is the diameter of the circle and $\pi \approx 3.14$. Notice that the diameter is twice the radius of the circle.

Example. The radius of a circle is 12.5 inches. What is its circumference?

Step 1. Apply the formula:

$$C = 2\pi \cdot r$$

$$C = 2 \cdot (3.14) \cdot (12.5) = 78.5$$

Step 2. So, the circumference is **78.5 inches.**

Area of Common Figures

Area is the amount of two-dimensional space inside a closed two-dimensional figure. A square with a side length of 1 unit, called **a unit square**, is said to have "one square unit" of area, and can be used to measure area.

A **square inch** is a unit of area equal to the area of a square with sides of one inch:

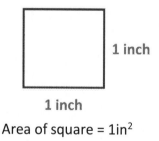

1 inch

1 inch

Area of square = $1in^2$

To find the area of a rectangle, multiply the length by the width:

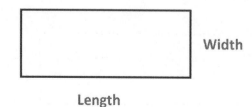

Width

Length

Area of rectangle = Length x Width

To find the area of a triangle, multiply the base by the height, then divide by 2.

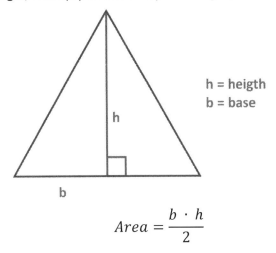

h = heigth
b = base

$$Area = \frac{b \cdot h}{2}$$

The base and height of a triangle must be **perpendicular** to each other.

To find the area of a square, multiply the side length by itself:

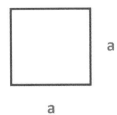

a

a

Area = a x a = a²

The area of a circle can be found by multiplying pi (π = 3.14) by the square of the radius. In other words, the area of a circle is given by the following formula:

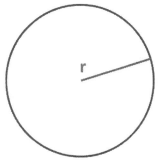

r

$$A = \pi \cdot r^2$$
$$r = radius$$

Example. Find the area of the rectangle:

7.6 in

13.4 in

Step 1. Apply the formula of the area of a rectangle:

$$Area = Length \cdot Width$$

$$Area = (13.4\ in.) \cdot (7.6\ in.) = \mathbf{101.84\ in^2}$$

Volume of Common Shapes

Volume is defined as the amount of space taken up by a three-dimensional object. Volume is expressed in **cubic units**, because it is the sum of three measurements (length, width, and depth) multiplied together. Cubic units include cm^3, m^3, cubic inches, and cubic feet.

A **cube** is a three-dimensional shape that has **squares** for all six of its sides. To find the volume of a cube, multiply the length by the width by the height:

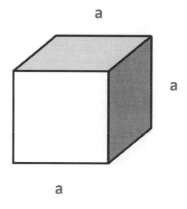

$$\boldsymbol{Volume = a \cdot a \cdot a = a^3}$$

To find the volume of a rectangular prism, multiply the length by the width by the height:

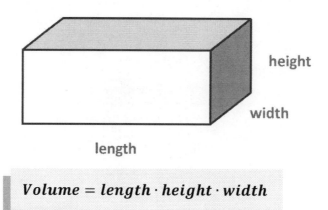

$$\boldsymbol{Volume = length \cdot height \cdot width}$$

To find the volume of a cylinder, multiply the area of the base (B) times the height (h):

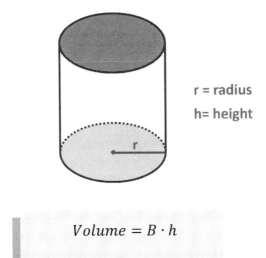

r = radius

h= height

$$Volume = B \cdot h$$

$$Volume = \pi \cdot r^2 \cdot h$$

The volume of a sphere is four-thirds times π times the radius cubed:

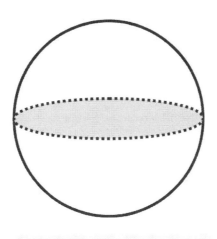

$$Volume = \frac{4}{3}\pi \cdot r^3$$

Example. Find the volume of the cylinder:

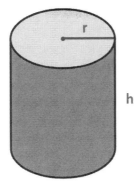

r = 15.5inches

h = 24 inches

Step 1. Apply the formula of the volume of the cylinder: (Recall that $\pi = 3.14$)

$$V = \pi \cdot r^2 \cdot h$$

$$V = 3.14 \cdot (15.5 \ in.)^2 \cdot 24 \ in.$$

$$V = 3.14 \cdot 240.25 \ in^2 \cdot 24 \ in. = \mathbf{18,105.24 \ in^3}$$

We can calculate area or volume of irregular or composite shapes by dividing the figure into smaller parts until we reach only shapes that we can work with easily.

Example. Find the area of this portion of a basketball court.

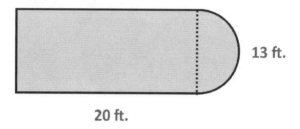

13 ft.

20 ft.

Step 1. Notice that the figure is formed by a rectangle and a semicircle (half of a circle). We need to find the area of each and add them together.

Step 2. Find the area of the rectangle:

$$A_1 = (20 \ ft) \cdot (13 \ ft) = 260 \ ft^2$$

Step 3. Find the area of the semicircle: (Note that the radius of the semicircle is 13/2 = 7.5 ft.)

$$A_2 = \frac{\pi \cdot r^2}{2} = \frac{3.14 \cdot (7.5 \ ft)^2}{2} = \frac{3.14 \cdot (56.25 \ ft^2)}{2} = 88.312 \ ft^2$$

Step 4. So, the area of the portion of the basketball court is:

$$A_T = A_1 + A_2 = 260 \ ft^2 + 88.312 \ ft^2 = \mathbf{348.312 \ ft^2}$$

Proportions

A proportion is a name we give to a statement in which two ratios are equal. It can be written as follows:

$$\frac{A}{B} = \frac{C}{D}$$

When two ratios are equal, the cross products of the ratios are equal:

$$\frac{A}{B} = \frac{C}{D}$$

$$\Rightarrow A \cdot D = B \cdot C$$

We can interpret and use proportions in solving problems involving dimensions or scale.

Example. A miniature model of a school is made using the scale 3 inch = 5 feet. If the height of the school is 19 feet, what is the height of the miniature model?

Step 1. Let x be the height of the miniature model.

Step 2. Write the proportion that represents the problem:

$$\frac{3\ inch}{5\ feet} = \frac{x}{19\ feet}$$

Step 3. Apply the cross products:

$$\frac{3\ inch}{5\ feet} = \frac{x}{19\ feet} \Rightarrow (5\ feet) \cdot x = (3\ inch) \cdot (19\ feet)$$

Step 4. We have an equation. Solve the equation:

$$(5\ feet) \cdot x = (3\ inch) \cdot (19\ feet)$$

$$\Rightarrow x = \frac{3\ inch \cdot 19\ feet}{5\ feet} = \frac{57\ inch \cdot feet}{5\ feet} = 11.4\ inches$$

Step 5. So, the height of the miniature model is **11.4 inches**.

Practice Exercises

1) How many minutes are in one week?

    A. 1,440
    B. 8,640
    C. 86,400
    D. 10,080

2) Which of the following is true?

    A. 1 week = 164 hours
    B. 540 seconds = 9 minutes
    C. 10 years = 126 months
    D. 2 days = 42 hours

3) Paul left home at 8:15 a.m. He jogged for 75 minutes. When did he return home?

    A. 9:30 a.m.
    B. 9:45 a.m.
    C. 10:05 a.m.
    D. 9:10 a.m.

4) The diameter of a circle is 30 inches. What is its circumference? (Use $\pi = 3.14$)

    A. 47.1 inches
    B. 56.5 inches
    C. 94.2 inches
    D. 96.6 inches

5) The circle below is inscribed in a square with a side length of 10 inches. What is the circumference of the circle? (Use $\pi = 3.14$)

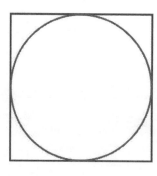

10 inches

    A. 15.7 inches
    B. 31.4 inches
    C. 78.5 inches
    D. 97.5 inches

6)   The area of a circle is 81π in². What is the radius of the circle?

   A.   81 inches

   B.   40.5 inches

   C.   27 inches

   D.   9 inches

7)   What is the approximate area of the following figure? (Use $\pi = 3.14$)

   A. 51
   B. 49
   C. 44.815
   D. 60

8)   What is the area of this room?

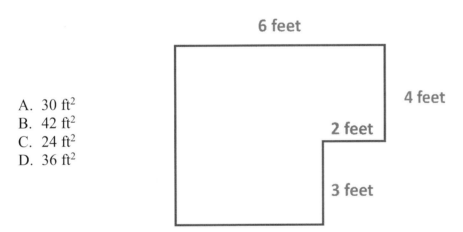

   A. 30 ft²
   B. 42 ft²
   C. 24 ft²
   D. 36 ft²

9)   If the circumference of a circle is 100π, what is the radius of the circle?

   A.   50

   B.   100

   C.   25

   D.   10

10) What is the volume of a sphere with a radius of 3 inches? (Use $\pi = 3.14$)

   A. 339.12 in³
   B. 169.56 in³
   C. 113.04 in³
   D. 94.17 in³

11) Nancy is allowed to watch 5.5 hours of television on Saturdays. Each episode of her favorite show lasts 30 minutes. How many episodes can she watch?

   A. 6
   B. 11
   C. 9
   D. 10

12) A tree is drawn using the scale 1 inch = 4 ft. If the tree is 11 inches in the drawing, how can we calculate the actual height of the tree?

   A. $\dfrac{1}{4} = \dfrac{x}{11}$

   B. $\dfrac{4}{x} = \dfrac{11}{1}$

   C. $\dfrac{1}{4} = \dfrac{11}{x}$

   D. $\dfrac{x}{4} = \dfrac{1}{11}$

13) A map of the city is made using the scale 2 inches = 14 feet. If the park in the city is 560 feet long, what is its length in the map?

   A. 80 inches
   B. 60 inches
   C. 72 inches
   D. 40 inches

14) Peter drew a picture of Lisa in his sketchbook using a scale of 3 cm = 1 foot. If Lisa is 5.5 feet tall, how tall is she in the drawing?

   A. 8.5 cm
   B. 15 cm
   C. 16.5 cm
   D. 18 cm

15) What is the volume of a cube with a side length of 1.5 feet?

    A. 2.25 ft^3

    B. 3.375 ft^3

    C. 4.55 ft^3

    D. 3.50 ft^3

ANSWER KEY

1) D	6) D	11) B
2) B	7) C	12) C
3) A	8) D	13) A
4) C	9) A	14) C
5) B	10) C	15) B

REFLECTION ON LEARNING

Answer the following reflection questions and feel free to discuss your responses with a classmate.

- What math idea, principle, or structure did you learn from this section?

  _____

  _____

  _____

  _____

- What math concepts did you learn?

  _____

  _____

  _____

  _____

- What procedures or method did you work on in this section?

  _____

  _____

  _____

  _____

- What aspect of this section is still not 100% clear for you?

  _____

  _____

  _____

  _____

- What else do you want your teacher to know?

  _____

  _____

  _____

  _____

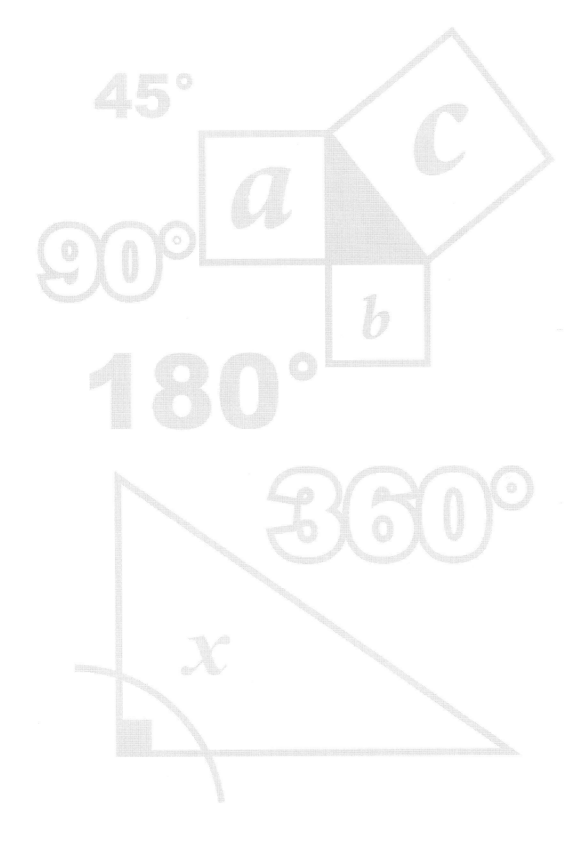

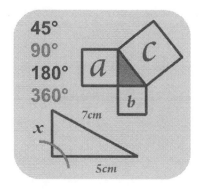

CHAPTER 5: GEOMETRY

KEY VOCABULARY

similarity, congruence, angle, triangle, complementary and supplementary angles, Pythagorean Theorem

Similarity and Congruence

Similar figures are the same shape as the real object but not the same size. The **scale factor** is **the ratio** of corresponding side lengths of similar figures.

Similar Figures

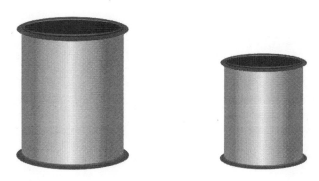

Example. Both rectangles below are similar. What is x?

Step 1. Since the rectangles are similar, we set up the proportion between corresponding side lengths:

$$\frac{5}{12} = \frac{14}{x}$$

Step 2. Solve the previous equation:

$$\frac{5}{12} = \frac{14}{x}$$

$$\Rightarrow 5x = (14) \cdot (12) \quad \text{(cross products)}$$

$$5x = 168$$

$$x = \frac{168}{5} = 33.6$$

Step 3. So, **x = 33.6 inches**. If one shape or geometric figure can become another using rotations, translations, or reflections, then the figures are **congruent**. When a figure is turned, it is called a **rotation**.

Rotation

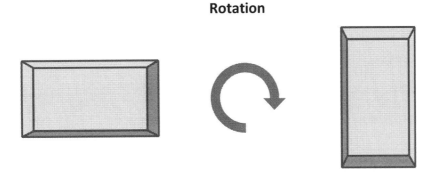

When a figure has been slid to a new location in space, it is called a **translation**.

Translation

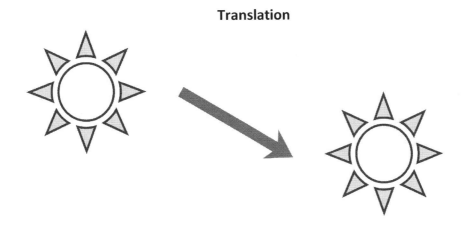

When a figure is flipped over a line, it is called a **reflection**.

Reflection

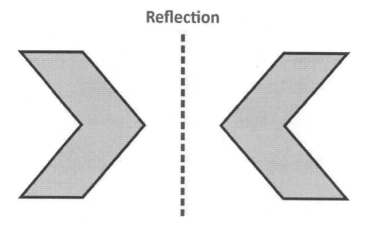

In other words, figures are congruent **when they are the same shape and size**, but have been flipped, slid, or turned.

Example. Which shape is not congruent to the other three?

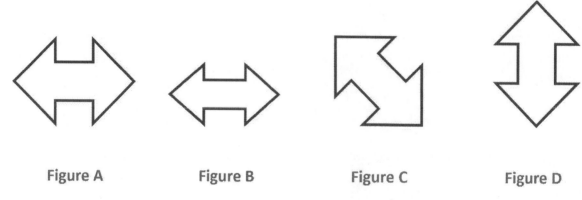

Figure A   Figure B   Figure C   Figure D

Step 1. Note that Figures A, C, and D have the same size, area, angles, and side lengths. Also, figures C and D are rotations of figure A. Figure B is similar to the other figures but does not have the same size or area.

Step 2. Thus, **figure B** is not congruent to the other figures.

Intersecting Lines

Intersecting lines are lines that share exactly one point. This shared point is called the **point of intersection**.

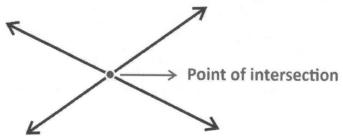

Point of intersection

When two lines intersect, they form two pairs of **opposite angles**. Another term for opposite angles is **vertical angles**. Vertical angles are always congruent, which means they are equal.

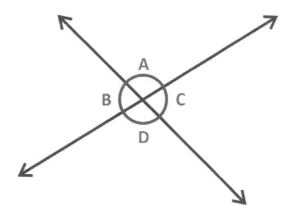

Vertical Angles: **Angle A = Angle D**

Vertical Angles: **Angle A = Angle D**

Complementary and Supplementary Angles

Two angles are complementary when they **add up to 90 degrees** (a right angle).

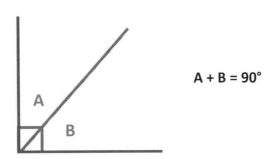

A + B = 90°

Two angles are supplementary when they add up to **180 degrees** (a straight angle).

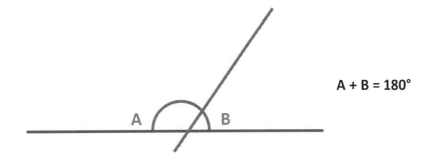

A + B = 180°

Example. What is the measure of angle x?

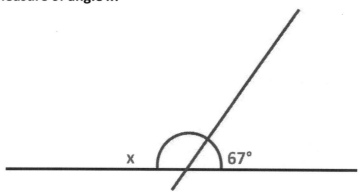

Step 1. Notice that the angle ABD and angle DBC are supplementary. Thus, we can set up the following equation:

$$x + 67° = 180°$$

Step 2. Solve the equation:

$$x + 67° = 180°$$

$$x = 180° - 67°$$

$$\mathbf{x = 113°}$$

Sexagesimal System

In sexagesimal system, the angle the rotating ray traces making one complete revolution is said to be 360°.One-fourth of it is 90° (a right angle) and 1/90th of a right angle is 1°. The other lower units of this system are *minute* and *second*.

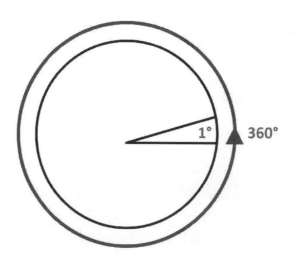

1° = 1/360th of revolution

360° = one complete revolution

We can set up the following relationships:

1 right angle = 90°

1° = 60 minutes or 60'

1' (one minute) = 60 seconds or 60"

Types of Shapes by Properties of Their Lines and Angles

Triangles

A triangle has three sides and three angles. The three angles always **add to 180°**.

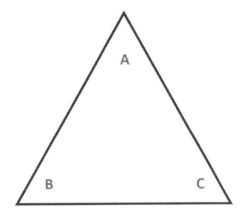

Angle A + Angle B + Angle C = 180°

There are three types of triangles based on the length of the sides:

Equilateral Triangle

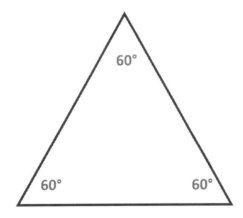

Three equal sides
Three equal angles, always **60°**

Isosceles Triangle

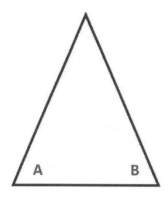

Two equal sides
Two equal angles
(Angle A = Angle B)

Scalene Triangle

No equal sides
No equal angles

There are three types of triangles based on the size of its inside angles:

Acute Triangle

All angles are **less than 90°**.

Right Triangle

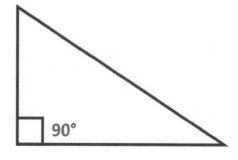

Has a right angle **(90°)**

Obtuse Triangle

Has an angle that is **more than 90°**

Example. What is the size of the missing angle X°?

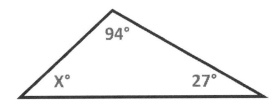

Step 1. We know that the three angles of a triangle always add to 180°. Thus, we can set up the following equation:

$$X + 94° + 27° = 180°$$

Step 2. Solve the equation:

$$X + 94° + 27° = 180°$$

$$X + 121° = 180°$$

$$X = 180° - 121°$$

$$\mathbf{X = 59°}$$

Quadrilaterals

A **quadrilateral** is a shape with four sides and four angles. The four angles always add to 360°.

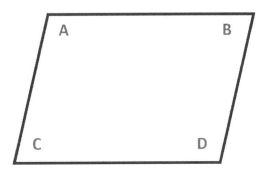

Angle A + Angle B + Angle C + Angle D = 360°

There are many types of quadrilaterals. A **parallelogram** is a quadrilateral in which both pairs of opposite sides are **parallel.**

A **rectangle** is a quadrilateral with four right angles. Thus, all rectangles are quadrilaterals and parallelograms:

A **square** is a quadrilateral with **4 equal sides** and every angle is a right angle (90°):

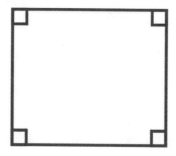

A **trapezoid** is a quadrilateral with exactly one pair of parallel sides:

A **kite** is a quadrilateral with exactly two pairs of adjacent congruent sides:

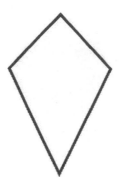

Pythagorean Theorem

The Pythagorean Theorem is a relationship between the sides in a right triangle. A **right triangle** is a triangle in which one of the three angles measures 90°. In a right triangle, the sides are called the **legs** and the **hypotenuse**.

The two legs meet at a 90° angle and the hypotenuse is the side opposite the right angle:

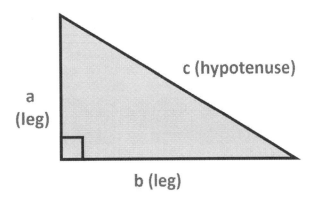

The Pythagorean Theorem says the following:

In a right triangle, the square of the hypotenuse is equal to the sum of the squares of the two legs.

This theorem can be written in one equation:

$$a^2 + b^2 = c^2$$

Example. The triangle below is a right triangle. Find x.

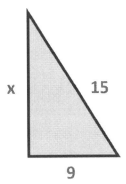

Step 1. Notice that x is the leg of the right triangle. Apply the Pythagorean Theorem:

$$a^2 + b^2 = c^2$$

$$x^2 + (9)^2 = (15)^2$$

$$x^2 + 81 = 225$$

Step 2. Solve the quadratic equation:

$$x^2 + 81 = 225$$

$$x^2 = 225 - 81$$

$$x^2 = 144$$

$$\Rightarrow x = \sqrt{144} = \mathbf{12}$$

PRACTICE EXERCISES

1) Triangle ABC is similar to triangle MNP. What is the measure of side MN?

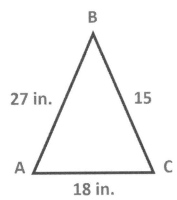
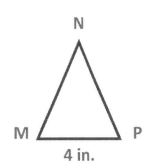

A. 8 in.
B. 6.5 in.
C. 9.3 in.
D. 6 in.

2) In the similar rectangles pictured below, what is x?

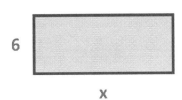
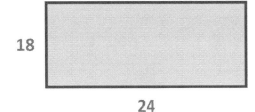

A. 8
B. 12
C. 10
D. 14.5

3) Rectangles A and B are congruent. What is the perimeter of rectangle B?

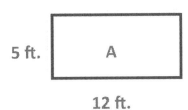

A. 17 ft.
B. 60 ft.
C. 34 ft.
D. 42 ft.

4)   The perimeter of an equilateral triangle is 63.3 inches. How long are its sides?

    A.   23 inches
    B.   21.1 inches
    C.   18.9 inches
    D.   There is not enough information given.

5) What is the measure of the angle A?

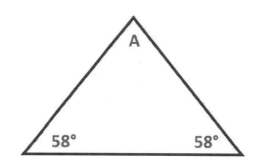

    A.   64°
    B.   58°
    C.   66°
    D.   71°

6)   What is the measure of the angle ABC?

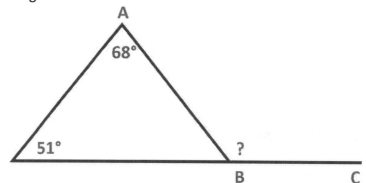

    A.   61°
    B.   123°
    C.   119°
    D.   108°

7)   What is the measure of angle M?

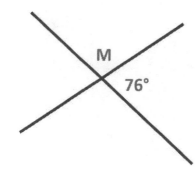

    A.   76°
    B.   104°
    C.   96°
    D.   114°

8) The measure of an angle is 38°. What is the measure of the complementary angle?

    A. 142°
    B. 72°
    C. 128°
    D. 52°

9) What is X?

    A. 32°
    B. 45°
    C. 19°
    D. 21°

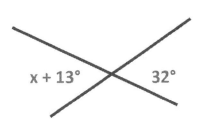

10) Two angles are complementary. One angle is 5 times larger than the other. What is the measure of the larger angle?

    A. 75°
    B. 80°
    C. 55°
    D. 15°

11) The measure of an angle is 80°. What is the measure of the supplementary angle?

    A. 10°
    B. 110°
    C. 100°
    D. 95°

12) Which of the following is true?

    A. The three angles of a triangle always add up to 360°.
    B. In a right triangle, the square of the hypotenuse is equal to the sum of the squares of the two legs.
    C. A trapezoid is a quadrilateral with exactly two pairs of parallel sides.
    D. Two figures are similar when they are the same shape and size.

13) The triangle below is a right triangle. What is the area of the square?

    A. 24 in^2
    B. 36 in^2
    C. 16 in^2
    D. 30 in^2

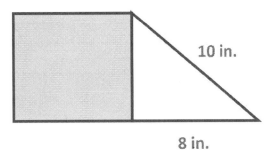

14) The following figure is formed by a right triangle and an equilateral triangle. What is the measure of angle x?

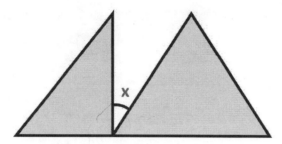

A. 60°
B. 45°
C. 30°
D. There is not enough information given.

15) What angle represents a half a revolution?

A. 90°
B. 360°
C. 180°
D. 45°

REFLECTION ON LEARNING

Answer the following reflection questions and feel free to discuss your responses with a classmate.

- What math idea, principle, or structure did you learn from this section?

  _____

  _____

  _____

- What math concepts did you learn?

  _____

  _____

  _____

- What procedures or method did you work on in this section?

  _____

  _____

  _____

- What aspect of this section is still not 100% clear for you?

  _____

  _____

  _____

- What else do you want your teacher to know?

  _____

  _____

  _____

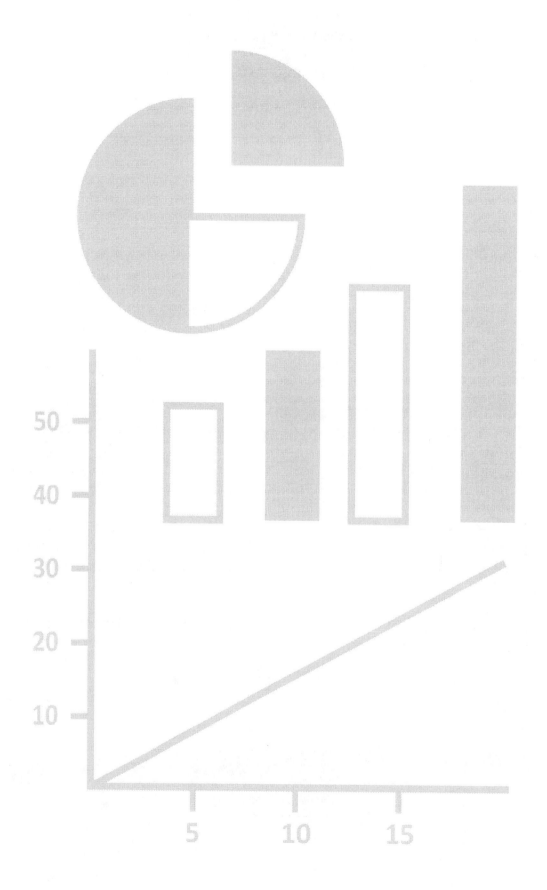

CHAPTER 6: STATISTICS, DATA ANALYSIS, AND PROBABILITY

KEY VOCABULARY

data set, chart, table, average, sample, linear model, event, probability

Center and Spread

When we talk about center or spread, we are talking about the **distribution** of data, or how data is spread across a graph or chart.

The **center** of a distribution is a measurement of what a **typical value** would be. We have two measurements for the center of a distribution, the **mean** and the **median.** The **mean** is the **average** of the numbers. To calculate the mean, we must add all the values and then divide by the total number of values in the data set. The **median** is the **middle** of a sorted list of numbers.

The **spread** is the measure of how far the numbers in a data set are away from the mean or median. The simplest way to find the spread in a data set is to identify the **range**, which is the difference between the highest and lowest values in the data set. The number that appears most often is called the **mode**.

An **outlier** is a portion of data that is an abnormal distance from other points. In other words, it is data that lies **outside the other values** in the set.

BOX PLOT

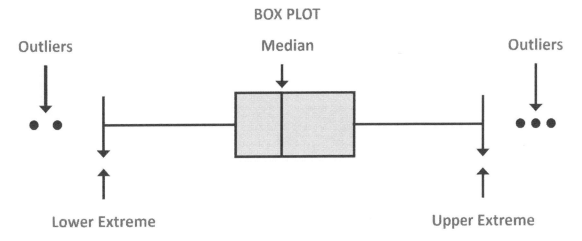

Example. Find the mean, median, and mode of the following data set:

$$15, 16, 15, 7, 21, 18, 19, 20, 15$$

Step 1. To calculate the mean, add together all the numbers in the set and then divide the sum by how many numbers there are. (In this case, there are 9 numbers.)

$$Mean = \frac{15 + 16 + 15 + 7 + 21 + 18 + 19 + 20 + 15}{9} = \frac{146}{9} = 16.22$$

Step 2. So, the mean is **16.22**

Step 3. To calculate the median, list the numbers from **smallest to largest**:

$$7, 15, 15, 15, 16, 18, 19, 20, 21$$

Step 4. Find the middle value of the data set:

$$7, 15, 15, 15, \mathbf{16}, 18, 19, 20, 21$$

Step 5. So, the median is **16**

Step 6. The mode is the value that occurs most often. Notice that 15 appear three times:

$$7, \mathbf{15, 15, 15}, 16, 18, 19, 20, 21$$

Step 7. So, the mode is **15**

Linear Model

A linear model is a comparison of two values, typically *x* and *y*, and the consistent change between the values. The consistent change is also known as the **rate of change.**

We can use the slope-intercept form, which is **y = mx + b**, to write equations for linear models. The slope or **rate of change** is **m**, and **b** is the y-intercept. The y-intercept represents **the starting point** of the equation.

Example. The following graph shows the relationship between the percentage of a battery's capacity (level of charge) and the time a battery is charging:

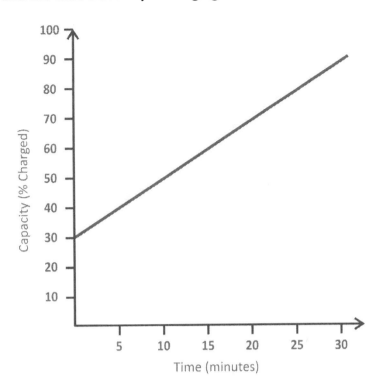

What was the battery's level of charge (% charged) when the charging began?

Step 1. Notice that the starting point of the line is **30** (y-axis). This value represents the y-intercept of the line. In this value, the time is zero (when the charging began).

Step 2. So, the battery's level of charge when the charging began was **30%**.

Probability of an Event

Probability is the **chance** that something will happen. The probability of an event is determined by dividing the favorable outcomes divided by the total number of outcomes. This means that probability is **always a number between 0 and 1**

We can see the mean of probability in the following scale:

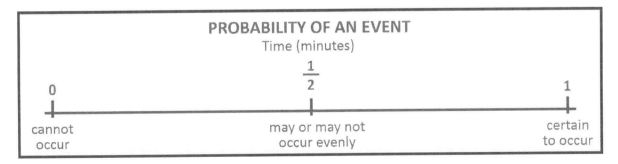

In other words, if an event has a 0 probability, that means it can never happen, because the favorable outcome is zero. If an event has a 1 probability, that means it will certainly happen, because there are the same number of favorable outcomes as there are total number of outcomes.

If an event has a ½ probability, it has an equal chance of happening or not happening. If an event has a probability between 0 and 0.5, then it is unlikely to happen, but not impossible. If an event has a probability between 0.5 and 1, then it is likely to happen, but not certain.

Probabilities can be expressed in terms of ratios. Since any ratio can be turned into a fraction, decimal, or percent, we can also turn any probability into a fraction, decimal, or percent. For example, the probability that a fair coin lands on heads is ½. This probability can be expressed in several forms:

$$P = \frac{1}{2}, \qquad P = 0.5, \qquad P = 50\%$$

Example. Find the probability of rolling an even number on a regular 6-sided die, and the probability of rolling an 8 on a regular 6-sided die.

Step 1. For the probability of rolling an even number, notice there are 3 odd numbers on a die (2, 4, 6), and there are a total of 6 possible outcomes (1, 2, 3, 4, 5, 6).

Step 2. Write the expression for the probability of rolling an odd number:

$$Probability = \frac{Number\ of\ ways\ it\ can\ happen}{Total\ number\ of\ outcomes} = \frac{3}{6} = \frac{1}{2}$$

Step 3. For the probability of rolling a 0, note that the number 8 does not appear on a regular 6-sided die. It is an impossible event. (That is, it cannot occur.)

Step 4. So, the probability of rolling an 8 on a regular 6-sided die is 0

PRACTICE EXERCISES

1)   The following graph shows the length of the Kevin´s beard (in millimeters) over time (weeks).

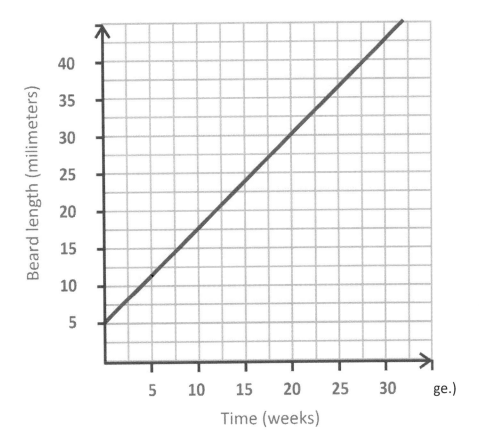

A.   3.5 millimeters per week

B.   3.0 millimeters per week

C.   1.25 millimeters per week

D.   2.25 millimeters per week

2)   What value occurs most often in a given data set?

A.   Mode

B.   Mean

C.   Median

D.   Outlier

3)   Which of the following events has a probability that equals 1?

A.   A head will come up in a coin toss.

B.   A tail will come up in a coin toss.

C.   A penguin will survive in the Sahara Desert.

D.   The sun will rise tomorrow.

4) A spinner has 5 equal sectors colored blue, green, red, brown, and yellow. What is the probability of landing on blue after spinning the spinner?

   A. 15%
   B. 25%
   C. 20%
   D. 45%

5) What is the probability of getting a number less than 5 when a die is rolled?

   A. 1/6
   B. 2/3
   C. 1/2
   D. 1/3

The box plot below summarizes the data for the average monthly high temperatures in degrees Fahrenheit for a city.

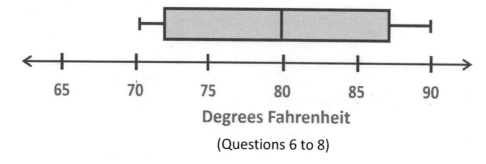

Degrees Fahrenheit

(Questions 6 to 8)

6) What is the minimum temperature recorded in the city?

   A. 65°F
   B. 70°F
   C. 75°F
   D. 80°F

7) What is the range of the data set?

   A. 20°F
   B. 80°F
   C. 70°F
   D. 25°F

8) What is the median of the data set?

   A. 75°F
   B. 85°F
   C. 80°F
   D. 60°F

9)   What is the slope of the linear model y = 6.82x + 0.2?

   A.   0.2
   B.   6.82
   C.   − 0.2
   D.   6.84

10)   What are the slope and y-intercept of the linear model $y = -10.77x$?

   A.   Slope = 0, intercept = −10.77
   B.   Slope = 1, intercept = 10.77
   C.   Slope = −10.77, intercept = 1
   D.   Slope = −10.77, intercept = 0

   Melissa normally makes really good grades in math class. Her test scores are 98, 95, 93, 99, 97, and 64. (Questions 11 to 12)

11)   Can the value 64 be considered an outlier?

   A.   Yes
   B.   No
   C.   There is not enough information given.

12)   What is the mean of her scores?

   A.   90.5
   B.   89.6
   C.   92.5
   D.   91

13)   What is the probability of choosing a vowel from the alphabet?

   A.   12/26
   B.   4/26
   C.   21/26
   D.   5/26

14)   What is the difference between the highest and lowest values in a data set called?

   A.   Mode
   B.   Range
   C.   Median
   D.   Average

15) What is the piece of data that is an abnormal distance from other points called?

A. Median
B. Rate of change
C. Outlier
D. Mean

ANSWER KEYS

1) C	6) B	11) A
2) A	7) A	12) D
3) D	8) C	13) D
4) C	9) B	14) B
5) B	10) D	15) C

REFLECTION ON LEARNING

Answer the following reflection questions and feel free to discuss your responses with a classmate.

- What math idea, principle, or structure did you learn from this section?

- What math concepts did you learn?

- What procedures or method did you work on in this section?

- What aspect of this section is still not 100% clear for you?

- What else do you want your teacher to know?

CHAPTER 7

PRACTICE TESTS

The real CASAS Math GOALS Form 918 M test has 40 items and is 75 minute long. So, to practice effectively learners should complete each practice test (40 test items) in 70 minutes. In other words, they will have 1 minute 45 seconds per math question.

Go to the next page to start practice test # 1.

MATH PRACTICE TEST # 1

40 Questions in 75 minutes

1) Which of the following is equivalent to 5%?

   A. 0.5
   B. 1/20
   C. 1/5
   D. 0.55

2) If Charlie runs 3.86 miles every day, how many miles will he run in 28 days?

   A. 98.68 miles
   B. 110.88 miles
   C. 80.8 miles
   D. 108.08 miles

3) A fisherman sold 18 pounds of shrimp and earned $129.60. How much does the shrimp cost per pound?

   A. $7.20
   B. $6.80
   C. $7.90
   D. $10.20

4) A train travels 1,442.25 miles in 4.5 hours. What is the average speed of the train?

   A. 350.6 miles per hour
   B. 290.5 miles per hour
   C. 320.5 miles per hour
   D. 330.8 miles per hour

5) Darrell earned 340 points on his exam. If he secured 85 % of the total points, what is the maximum number of points he could have earned on the exam?

   A. 400
   B. 450
   C. 380
   D. 425

6) Which of the following is equivalent to 3/5?

    A. 55%
    B. 80%
    C. 70%
    D. 60%

7) A company took a survey about its new product. Of the 300 people surveyed, 70% liked the new product. How many people liked the new product?

    A. 230
    B. 210
    C. 215
    D. 190

8) Daniel can grow 15 plants with every seed packet. Which of the following equations shows the relationship between the number of seed packets, x, and the total number of plants, y?

    A. $x = y + 15$
    B. $y = x + 15$
    C. $15y = x$
    D. $y = 15x$

9) A 9-inch by 12-inch picture is placed in a frame that creates a uniform border of n inches around the picture, as shown below. The area of the entire frame (including where the picture is placed) is equal to 214 square inches. What is the equation that finds the value of n?

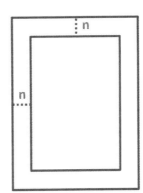

    A. $(n + 9)(n + 12) = 214$
    B. $2n + 9 + 12 = 214$
    C. $(9 + 2n)(12 + 2n) = 214$
    D. $9n + 12n = 214$

10) The formula for converting a measurement in Fahrenheit to Kelvin is: $F = 1.8K - 459.67$, where F is the temperature in degrees Fahrenheit and K is the temperature in degrees Kelvin. If the temperature is 90 degrees Fahrenheit, what is it in Kelvin?

    A. 305.372°K
    B. 456.98°K
    C. 205.372°K
    D. 333.372°K

11) The sum of three consecutive numbers is 240. What is the largest of the three numbers?

   A. 84
   B. 79
   C. 81
   D. 93

12) Billy was selling tickets for the school play. He sold 20 more adult tickets than children tickets and he sold twice as many senior tickets as children tickets. Adult tickets cost $6, children's tickets cost $2, and senior tickets cost $3. Billy made $540.How many adult tickets were sold?

   A. 60
   B. 50
   C. 48
   D. 32

13) What is the missing term in the following sequence?

$$4, 16, 64, \underline{\quad}, 1024, ...$$

   A. 164
   B. 356
   C. 518
   D. 256

14) If the ratio of boys to girls in a school is 7:9 and the number of boys is 189, how many girls are in the school?

   A. 243
   B. 199
   C. 343
   D. 208

15) If Catherine can type 540 pages of manuscript in 20 days, how many days will it take her to type 810 pages if she works at the same rate?

   A. 25
   B. 32
   C. 30
   D. 29

16) What is the missing value in the following table of equivalent ratios?

14	77
20	110
?	176

A. 46
B. 32
C. 28
D. 36

17) There are 418students in a school. The ratio of boys to girls in this school is 4:7. How many girls are in the school?

A. 258
B. 266
C. 152
D. 187

18) The ratio of girls to boys in a bicycling club is5:6. There are48 boys. How many total members are there in the club?

A. 88
B. 76
C. 92
D. 85

19) The following table shows Lisa's earnings based on the number of hours she works:

Number of hours	5	10	12
Lisa's earnings	$60	$120	$140

Are Lisa's earnings proportional to the number of hours she works?

A. Yes
B. No
C. There is not enough information given.
D. None of the above

20) Which of the following is true?

    A. 10 years = 115 months
    B. 10 weeks = 60 days
    C. 20 minutes = 1,500 seconds
    D. 0.5 hour = 30 minutes

21) Ashley left home at 9:30 a.m. She walked for 90 minutes. When did she return home?

    A. 10:30 a.m.
    B. 11.00 a.m.
    C. 11:15 a.m.
    D. 10:45 a.m.

22) The radius of a circle is 100 inches. What is its circumference? (Use $\pi = 3.14$)

    A. 628 inches
    B. 314 inches
    C. 62.8 inches
    D. 31.5 inches

23) The circumference of a circle is 4π feet. What is its radius?

    A. 4 feet
    B. 3.14 feet
    C. 2 feet
    D. 2.5 feet

24) The area of the rectangle below is 180 in^2. What is x?

    A. 14 inches
    B. 12 inches
    C. 9 inches
    D. 16 inches

x

15 inches

25) The area of the shaded triangle is 29 in^2. What is the area of the rectangle?

    A. 44 in^2
    B. 39 in^2
    C. 14.5 in^2
    D. 58 in^2

26) A light pole is drawn using the scale 1 inch = 3 ft. If the light pole is 14 inches in the drawing, how can we calculate the actual height of the light pole?

A. $\frac{1}{3} = \frac{x}{14}$

B. $\frac{1}{3} = \frac{14}{x}$

C. $\frac{3}{x} = \frac{14}{1}$

D. $\frac{x}{14} = \frac{3}{1}$

27) John's room has a length of 20 feet. In the map, his room is 4 in long. What is the scale used in the map?

A. 1 in. = 5 ft.
B. 5 in. = 1 ft.
C. 1 in. = 4 ft.
D. 1ft. = 50 in.

28) What is the approximate volume of the following figure? (Use $\pi = 3.14$)

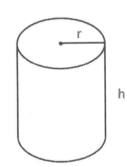

A. 848 ft³
B. 3,815 ft³
C. 4,563 ft³
D. 1,696 ft³

r = 9 feet
h= 15 feet

29) In the similar rectangles pictured below, what is x?

9.6

x

A. 3.3
B. 4.2
C. 1.8
D. 2.4

6.5

26

30) Rectangles A and B are congruent. What is the area of the rectangle B?

A. 31 ft²
B. 43 ft²
C. 52 ft²
D. 57 ft²

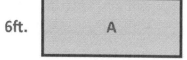 

6ft.

9.5ft.

31) What is the measure of the angle X?

A. 84
B. 76°
C. 94°
D. 100°

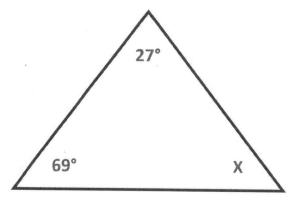

27°

69°

X

32) The measure of an angle is 53°. What is the measure of the supplementary angle?

A. 37°
B. 41°
C. 127°
D. 132°

33) What angle represents a quarter of a revolution?

A. 25°
B. 45°
C. 60°
D. 90°

34) What is X?

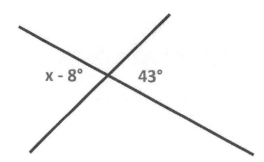

x - 8°   43°

A. 35°
B. 54°
C. 51°
D. 49°

35) What is the height we can reach with a 10-foot ladder leaning against a wall if the bottom of the ladder is 6 feet from the wall?

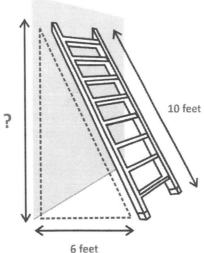

A. 7 feet
B. 5.5 feet
C. 8 feet
D. 6 feet

36) The following data represents the height in inches of a volleyball team. What is the median height of the team?

80   78   77   82   83   83   81   79   79   77   76   81   79   80   80

A. 81 inches
B. 79 inches
C. 82.5 inches
D. 80 inches

37) A college professor asked his students to complete a personality test. He paid special attention to his students' career goals and their greatest fears. The results are shown in this table:

	Doctor	Lawyer
Fear of spiders	20	18
Fear of the dark	30	12

What is the probability that a randomly selected student has a fear of dark and wants to be a doctor?

A. 3/8

B. 2/5

C. 9/15

D. 3/4

38) A number from 1 to 15 is chosen at random. What is the probability of choosing an even number?

A. 6/15

B. 4/15

C. 7/15

D. 2/15

39) Which of these numbers cannot be a probability?

A. 0.74

B. 17%

C. 6/5

D. 0.05

40) What is the probability of getting a number less than 3 when a die is rolled?

A. 1/2

B. 1/3

C. 1/6

D. 1/5

REFLECTION ON PRACTICE TEST # 1

Answer the following reflection questions and feel free to discuss your responses with your teacher or a classmate.

- How do you feel about your performance on the practice test?

- Was anything too hard for you? What was it?

- Was anything too easy for you? What was it?

- What math procedures do you still need to review?

- List the math procedures and skills that you need to work on or to practice more.

- What else do you want your teacher to know?

MATH PRACTICE TEST # 2

40 Questions in 70 minutes

1) Which of the following is equivalent to 0.75?

   A. 7.5%
   B. 75%
   C. 0.75%
   D. 1.75%

2) For a school party, the principal bought 28 big bags of candy. There were 3,785 pieces of candy in each bag. How many pieces of candy did the principal buy in total?

   A. 115,670
   B. 104,970
   C. 105,980
   D. 201,990

3) If Jessica runs 2 miles every day, how many miles will she run in 5.5days?

   A. 11 miles
   B. 10 miles
   C. 12.5 miles
   D. 9.5 miles

4) 1,348 people were transported in buses that carry 25 passengers each. How many buses were needed?

   A. 53
   B. 48
   C. 60
   D. 54

5) On a math test, Raul correctly answered 32 questions. These correct answers gave him a score of 64%. In total, how many questions were on his math test?

   A. 60
   B. 45
   C. 50
   D. 55

6) In an election, Mr. Stevenson got 75% of the total valid votes. Of the total votes, 20% were declared invalid. If the total number of votes is 800, what is the number of valid votes in favor of Mr. Stevenson?

    A. 640
    B. 480
    C. 520
    D. 600

7) What is the result of $0.25 + \frac{1}{2}$?

    A. 3/4
    B. 2/5
    C. 4/3
    D. 1/3

8) Which equation represents the phrase, "Nine less than x is equal to 58"?

    A. $9 - x = 58$
    B. $x - 58 = 9$
    C. $9x = 58$
    D. $x - 9 = 58$

9) Which equation represents the phrase, "Four more than five times a number is forty-six"?

    A. $4x + 5 = 46$
    B. $5x + 4 = 46$
    C. $5x + 46 = 4$
    D. $x + 5 = 46$

10) Mia collects t-shirts. She has 13t-shirts already and buys3 more shirts each week. How many weeks would it take her to collect 61 t-shirts?

    A. 16
    B. 14
    C. 21
    D. 18

11) Ralph has a total of 163 coins in his coin collection. This is 15 more than four times the number of quarters in the collection. How many quarters does Ralph have in his collection?

    A. 19
    B. 34
    C. 37
    D. 40

12) What is the missing term in the following sequence?

$$4{,}375, \quad 875, \quad \underline{}, \quad 35, \quad 7, \dots$$

    A.   155
    B.   305
    C.   175
    D.   495

13) Consider the following formula: $P_E = m \cdot g \cdot h$

Where P_E represents the potential energy of an object,

M represents the mass of the object and has units of kilograms (*kg*),

g represents the acceleration of gravity and has units of meters per second per second $\left(\frac{m}{s^2}\right)$, and

h represents the height of the object and has units of meters (*m*).

Which of the following is an appropriate measurement unit for potential energy?

    A. $\dfrac{kg \cdot m^2}{s^2}$

    B. $\dfrac{kg \cdot m}{s^2}$

    C. $\dfrac{s \cdot m^2}{kg^2}$

    D. $kg \cdot m^2/s$

14) What is the missing value in the following table of equivalent ratios?

9	81
13	117
?	261

    A.   29
    B.   27
    C.   21
    D.   30

15) Vanessa can make 28 sandwiches in 1hour. Assuming she works at this constant rate, how many complete sandwiches can she make in 95 minutes?

A. 40
B. 45
C. 51
D. 44

16) The currency in Italy is the euro. If we exchange $385 at the airport, how many euros will we get in return? (1 euro = 1.10 dollars)

A. 423.5 euros
B. 350 euros
C. 310 euros
D. 393 euros

17) Steve wants to give a party for 80 people. He has a punch recipe that makes 3.5 gallons of punch and serves 20 people. How many gallons of punch should he make for his party?

A. 12.5 gallons
B. 15 gallons
C. 14 gallons
D. 13.5 gallons

18) A copy machine can make 3,600 copies in an hour. How many copies can it make per minute?

A. 45
B. 50
C. 60
D. 72

19) Which of the following is true?

A. 2 weeks = 336 hours
B. 5 hours = 360 minutes
C. 14,000 seconds = 4 hours
D. 2 hours = 7,400 seconds

20) The ratio of girls to boys in a science club is 6 : 7. There are 78 girls. How many total members are there in the club?

A. 159
B. 169
C. 158
D. 170

21) The diameter of a circle is 50 inches. What is its circumference? (Use $\pi = 3.14$)

    A. 78.5 inches

    B. 80 inches

    C. 155.5 inches

    D. 157 inches

22) The circle below is inscribed in a square with side length 4.5 feet. What is the circumference of the circle? (Use $\pi = 3.14$)

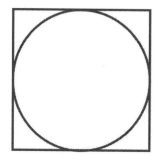

    A. 7.065 feet

    B. 12.66 feet   4,5 feet

    C. 20.5 feet

    D. 14.13 feet

23) The area of the triangle below is 71.5 in². What the height of the triangle?

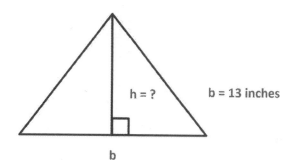

h = ?   b = 13 inches

    A. 10 inches.

    B. 11 inches

    C. 15.5 inches   b

    D. 18 inches

24) A water storage tank consists of a cylinder capped with a hemisphere as shown below. What is the approximate volume of the storage tank? (Use $\pi = 3.14$)

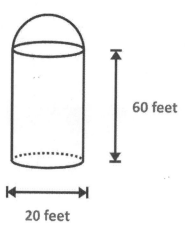

    A. 20,933 ft³

    B. 79,546 ft³

    C. 41,100 ft³   60 feet

    D. 34,635 ft³

20 feet

25) Triangle MNP is similar to triangle RST:

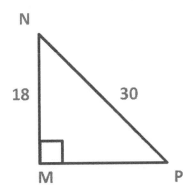
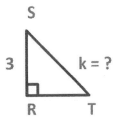

What is the value of k?

A. 4
B. 6.5
C. 5
D. 7

26) What is the volume of a cube with a side length of 10inches?

A. 100 in^3
B. 1,000 in^3
C. 500 in^3
D. 1,500 in^3

27) Jennifer's room has a length of 29 feet. On a map, her room is 14.5 in long. What is the scale used in the map?

A. 1 inch = 2 feet
B. 1 feet = 2 inches
C. 1 inch. = 2.5 feet
D. 2 inch = 4.5 inches

28) Which triangle is congruent to triangle A?

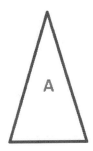

Triangle 1

Triangle 2

Triangle 3

Triangle 4

A. Triangle 4
B. Triangle 1
C. Triangle 3
D. Triangle 2

29) What is the measure of the angle B?

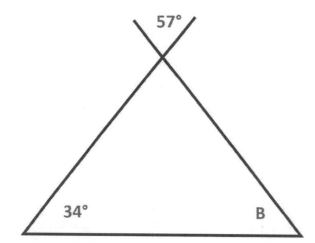

A.   68°
B.   91°
C.   89°
D.   79°

30) Two angles are supplementary and one of them is 88°. What is the size of the other angle?

A.   2°
B.   92°
C.   84°
D.   12°

31) Which pair of angles are complementary?

A.   60°, 120°
B.   18°, 62°
C.   45°, 50°
D.   34°, 56°

32)   What is X?

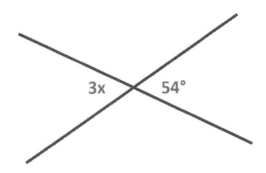

$3x$ $54°$

A.   18°
B.   36°
C.   15°
D.   17°

33)   What angle represents two revolutions?

A.   540°
B.   270°
C.   720°
D.   360°

34)   Look at the following dot plot:

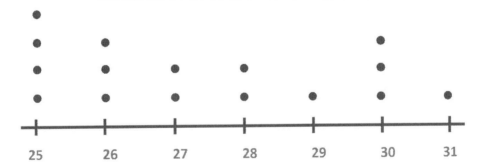

NUMBER OF STUDENTS PER CLASSROOM

25   26   27   28   29   30   31

What is the median of the number of students?

A.   28
B.   27
C.   30
D.   26

35)   Look at the following box plot:

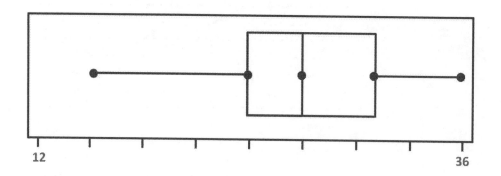

What is the median of the data set?

    A.   25

    B.   30

    C.   27

    D.   29

36)   The data below are the number of points scored by a basketball team over its last 15 games:

62, 57, 63, 65, 68, 63, 63, 72, 80, 66, 65, 73, 71, 77, 63

What is the range of the data set?

    A.   31

    B.   20

    C.   23

    D.   21

37)   There are 12 green and 18 blue marbles in a bag. If one marble is chosen at random, what is the probability of getting a blue marble?

    A.   0.60

    B.   0.55

    C.   0.75

    D.   1.30

The following graph represents a linear model: (Questions 38 to 40)

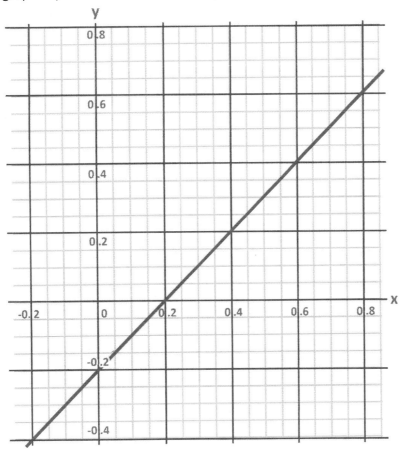

38) What is the slope for this linear model?

   A. − 1
   B. 1
   C. 0.2
   D. − 0.2

39) What is the intercept for this linear model?

   A. 0.2
   B. − 0.2
   C. 0.4
   D. 1.6

40) What is the equation that represents the linear model?

   A. $y = x - 0.1$
   B. $y = 0.2 - x$
   C. $y = x + 0.2$
   D. $y = x - 0.2$

REFLECTION ON PRACTICE TEST # 2

Answer the following reflection questions and feel free to discuss your responses with your teacher or a classmate.

- How do you feel about your performance on the practice test?

- Was anything too hard for you? What was it?

- Was anything too easy for you? What was it?

- What math procedures do you still need to review?

- List the math procedures and skills that you need to work on or to practice more.

- What else do you want your teacher to know?

$$-\frac{y^2}{z} = 2\sqrt{\frac{(x^a - y^b)(3z+2)}{a^3 + b^2}}$$

$$\frac{+\frac{1}{2}b^x}{y^2} \qquad \frac{z^3}{a^3} = \frac{(a^2 + b^2 + x^2 + y^2)}{\sqrt{3x - 2y^3 -}}$$

$$\frac{(2xy)^2 (3ab + 3x)^3}{x^3 y^2} = \frac{5x^2 + 3}{z^2 c}$$

$$\downarrow f(x) \qquad \iint_0 dx\,dy \int_0^{1-x-y} \frac{dz}{(x+y.}$$

$$\left(\frac{1}{(x+y+1)^2} - \frac{1}{2} \right) dy = \frac{1}{2} \left(l_n \right.$$

PRACTICE TEST ANSWER KEYS

PRACTICE TEST #1

1) B	9) C	17) B	25) D	33) D
2) D	10) A	18) A	26) B	34) C
3) A	11) C	19) B	27) A	35) C
4) C	12) B	20) D	28) B	36) D
5) A	13) D	21) B	29) D	37) A
6) D	14) A	22) A	30) D	38) C
7) B	15) C	23) C	31) A	39) C
8) D	16) B	24) B	32) C	40) B

PRACTICE TEST #2

1) B	9) B	17) C	25) C	33) C
2) C	10) A	18) C	26) B	34) B
3) A	11) C	19) A	27) A	35) C
4) D	12) C	20) B	28) D	36) C
5) C	13) A	21) D	29) C	37) A
6) B	14) A	22) D	30) B	38) B
7) A	15) D	23) B	31) D	39) B
8) D	16) B	24) A	32) A	40) D

ABOUT COACHING FOR BETTER LEARNING, LLC

CBL helps develop systems that increase performance and save time, resources, and energy.

If you identify typos and errors in the text, please let us know at coachingforbetterlearning@gmail.com. We promise to fix them and send you a free copy of the updated textbook to thank you.

Made in the USA
Middletown, DE
12 April 2021